Preface

This book "MySQL Lab Manual" is your companion on a journey through the intricate and dynamic world of MySQL, an open-source relational database management system that has captivated the hearts of developers, database administrators, and businesses worldwide.

In a data-driven era where information is the lifeblood of organizations, mastering a robust and versatile database system like MySQL is of paramount importance. This book is tailored to meet the diverse needs of readers, whether you're taking your first steps into the realm of databases or you're an experienced database professional looking to deepen your MySQL expertise.

As you navigate through these pages, you'll find the collective wisdom of experienced database professionals, developers, and MySQL enthusiasts who have contributed to this comprehensive resource.

We'd like to express our gratitude to the MySQL community, whose passion and dedication have played an instrumental role in shaping this book. We'd also like to thank our families, friends, and colleagues for their unwavering support throughout this endeavour.

We believe that this book will be a valuable resource on your journey to becoming a MySQL master. Whether you're a student, a professional, or an enthusiast, we hope this book equips you with the knowledge and skills you need to harness the full potential of MySQL.

Table of Contents

Chapter 1 : Introduction to MySQL

Overview of MySQL

What is MySQL?
MySQL stands as the leading open-source relational database management system (RDBMS), fostered, distributed, and supported by Oracle Corporation. It's pivotal for managing structured data across various applications and systems. The MySQL website (http://www.mysql.com/) provides the latest information about MySQL software.

Relational Database System:
MySQL employs a relational structure, organizing data into distinct tables for efficient storage. It optimizes database structures into physical files for enhanced speed, offering a logical model comprising databases, tables, views, and more, providing a flexible programming environment.
Structured Query Language (SQL):
MySQL integrates SQL, the standard language for interacting with databases. It allows direct SQL inputs, embedding SQL within code, or using language-specific APIs to access and manipulate data stored in the database.
Open-Source Nature:
MySQL embodies an open-source ethos, allowing unrestricted usage and modifications. Anyone can freely download, study, and modify the MySQL software due to its GNU General Public License (GPL). A commercially licensed version is also available for embedding MySQL code in commercial applications.
Performance and Reliability:
Recognized for its speed, reliability, scalability, and ease of use, MySQL operates proficiently across diverse environments. From single desktop installations to clustered configurations, it adapts to available hardware resources and sustains high-performance levels.
Client/Server Architecture:
MySQL operates as a client/server system, comprising a multithreaded SQL server, client programs, libraries, administrative tools, and a range of application programming interfaces (APIs). Additionally, it offers an embedded library suitable for integration into applications.
MySQL HeatWave:
MySQL HeatWave introduces a fully managed database service, leveraging the HeatWave in-memory query accelerator. It integrates transactions, real-time analytics across data warehouses and lakes, and machine learning within a unified MySQL Database, minimizing complexities and costs associated with data duplication.
MySQL HeatWave is available across Oracle Cloud Infrastructure (OCI), AWS, and Azure. For more information, visit Oracle's MySQL page.

Main Features of MySQL

Internals and Portability:
Written in C and C++: MySQL is primarily developed using C and C++ languages, ensuring efficiency and performance.
Example: Understanding MySQL's core programming languages can help in optimizing queries and performance tuning.
Multi-Platform Support: MySQL is designed to operate on various platforms, ensuring compatibility across different systems.
Example: Installing and running MySQL on Windows, Linux, or macOS to showcase its cross-platform capabilities.
Scalability and Limits:
Support for Large Databases: MySQL accommodates extensive datasets, showcasing its capability to handle substantial records and tables.
Example: Creating and populating a database with millions of records to demonstrate MySQL's scalability.
Indexing: MySQL supports multiple indexes per table, aiding in faster data retrieval.
Example: Creating different indexes on a table and comparing query performance with and without indexes.
Connectivity:
Diverse Client Connections: MySQL allows clients to connect via various protocols such as TCP/IP, named pipes, and Unix domain sockets.

Example: Connecting MySQL clients using TCP/IP sockets and Unix domain sockets to demonstrate diverse connectivity options.
APIs and Interfaces: MySQL offers APIs and interfaces for languages like Java, Python, PHP, and others for seamless integration.
Example: Developing a simple application using MySQL Connector/J in Java to perform database operations.
Localization:
Language Support: MySQL supports multiple languages for error messages and different character sets.
Example: Configuring MySQL to display error messages in different languages and using various character sets.
Collation and Sorting: MySQL allows changing collation for sorting based on different character sets.
Example: Sorting and comparing data using different collations for specific character sets.
Clients and Tools:
Command-Line Utilities: MySQL provides various command-line tools for database administration and maintenance.
Example: Using utilities like **mysqladmin** or **mysqldump** to perform tasks such as backup, restore, and table maintenance.
Graphical Tools: MySQL Workbench offers a graphical interface for database design, modeling, and administration.
Example: Creating ER diagrams or performing database modeling using MySQL Workbench.

In a MySQL Lab Manual, these detailed features can be accompanied by step-by-step exercises, hands-on tasks, and practical examples to familiarize learners with MySQL's capabilities. Practical demonstrations and exercises provide a hands-on approach, reinforcing theoretical concepts and aiding in practical application and understanding.

Installation and Setup

MySQL is one of the most popular relational database management software that is widely used in today's industry. It provides multi-user access support with various storage engines. It is backed by Oracle Company. In this section, we are going to learn how we can download and install MySQL for beginners.

Prerequisites

The following requirements should be available in your system to work with MySQL:

MySQL Setup Software
Microsoft .NET Framework 4.5.2
Microsoft Visual C++ Redistributable for Visual Studio 2019
RAM 4 GB (6 GB recommended)

Download MySQL

Follow these steps:

Step 1: Go to the official website (https://dev.mysql.com/downloads/installer/) of MySQL and download the community server edition software. Here, you will see the option to choose the Operating System, such as Windows.
Step 2: Next, there are two options available to download the setup. Choose the version number for the MySQL community server, which you want. If you have good internet connectivity, then choose the mysql-installer-web-community. Otherwise, choose the other one.

Installing MySQL on Windows

Step 1: After downloading the setup, unzip it anywhere and double click the MSI **installer .exe file.** It will give the following screen:

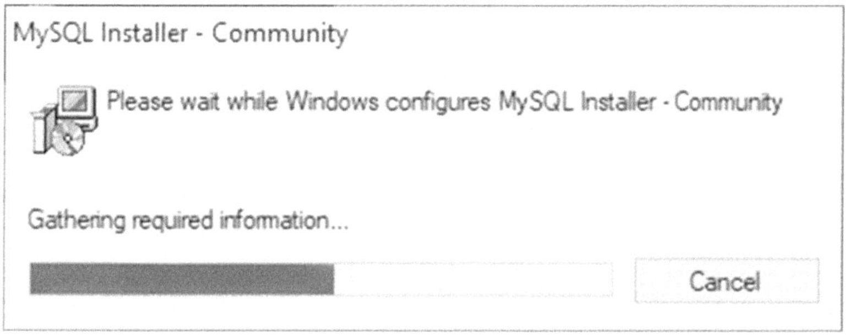

Step 2: In the next wizard, choose the **Setup Type**. There are several types available, and you need to choose the appropriate option to install MySQL product and features. Here, we are going to select the **Full** option and click on the Next button.

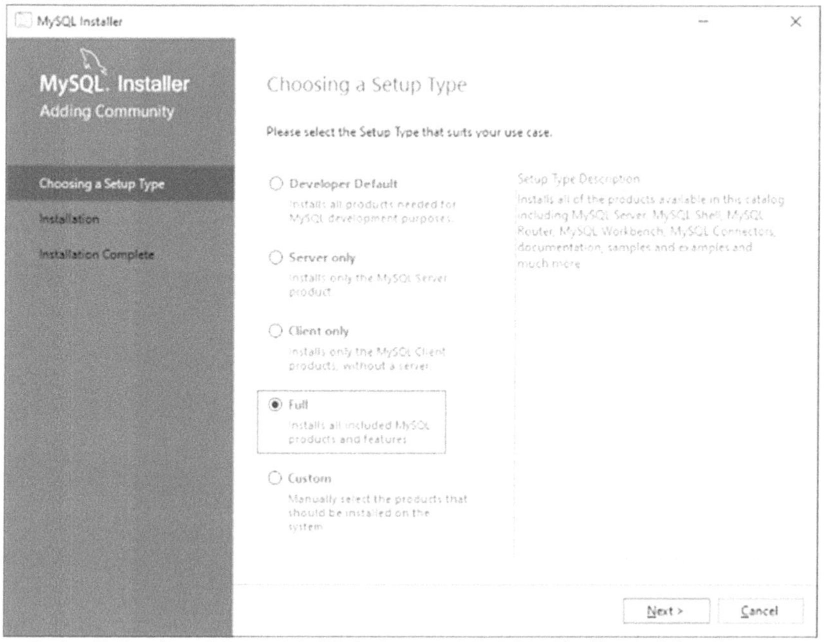

This option will install the following things: MySQL Server, MySQL Shell, MySQL Router, MySQL Workbench, MySQL Connectors, documentation, samples and examples, and many more.

Step 3: Once we click on the Next button, it may give information about some features that may fail to install on your system due to a lack of requirements. We can resolve them by clicking on the **Execute** button that will install all requirements automatically or can skip them. Now, click on the Next button.

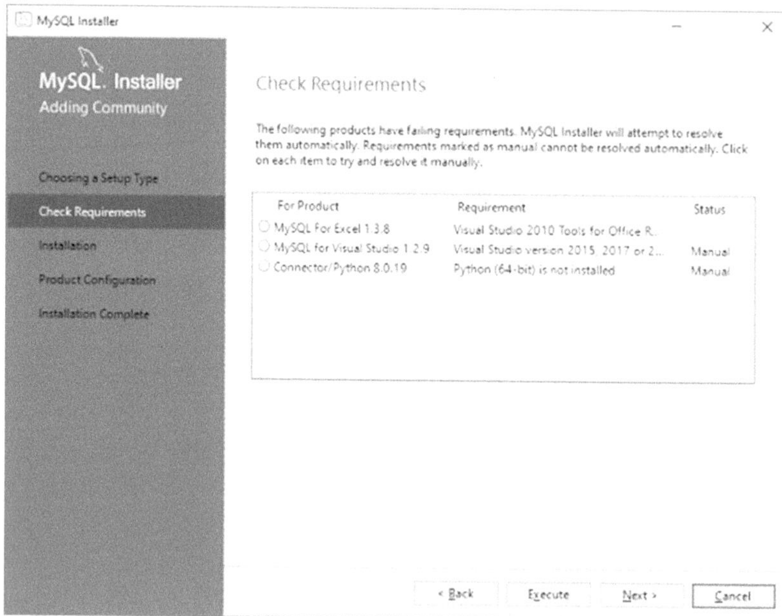

Step 4: In the next wizard, we will see a dialog box that asks for our confirmation of a few products not getting installed. Here, we have to click on the **Yes** button.

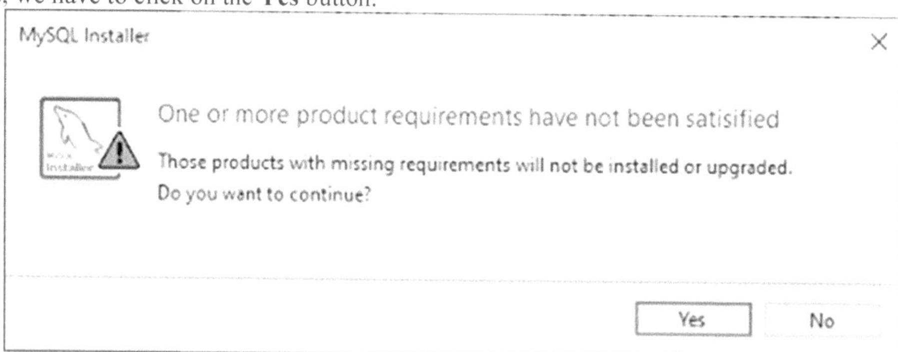

After clicking on the Yes button, we will see the list of the products which are going to be installed. So, if we need all products, click on the Execute button.

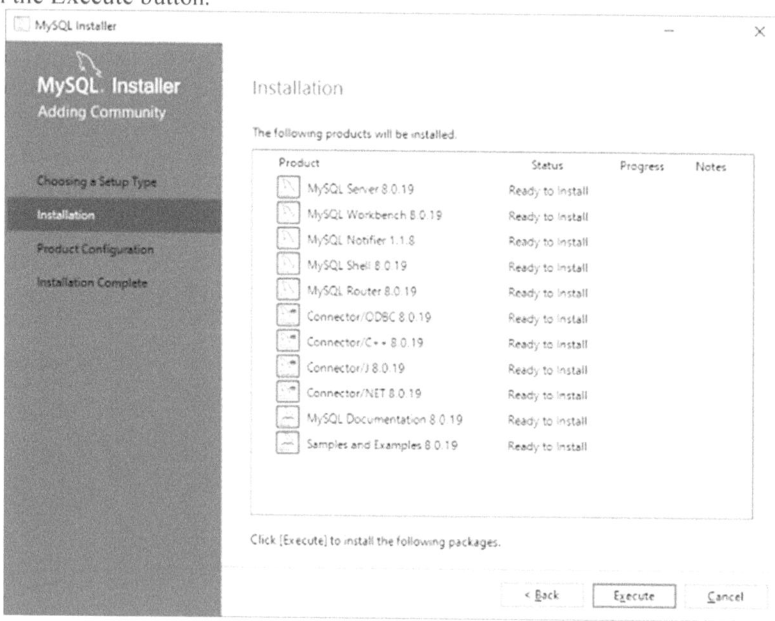

Step 5: Once we click on the Execute button, it will download and install all the products. After completing the installation, click on the Next button.

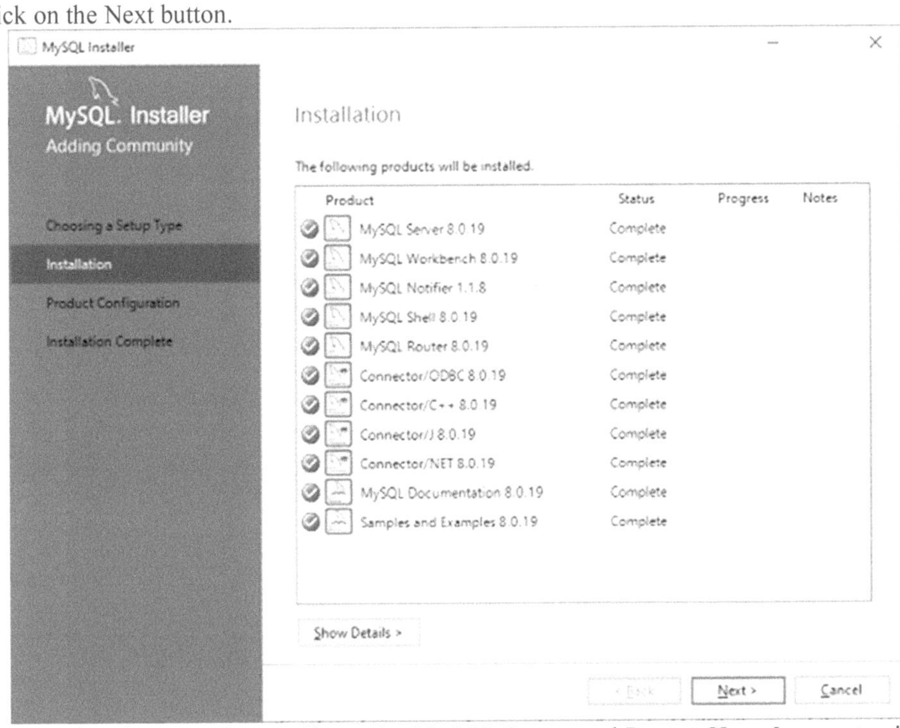

Step 6: In the next wizard, we need to configure the MySQL Server and Router. Here, I am not going to configure the Router because there is no need to use it with MySQL. We are going to show you how to configure the server only. Now, click on the Next button.

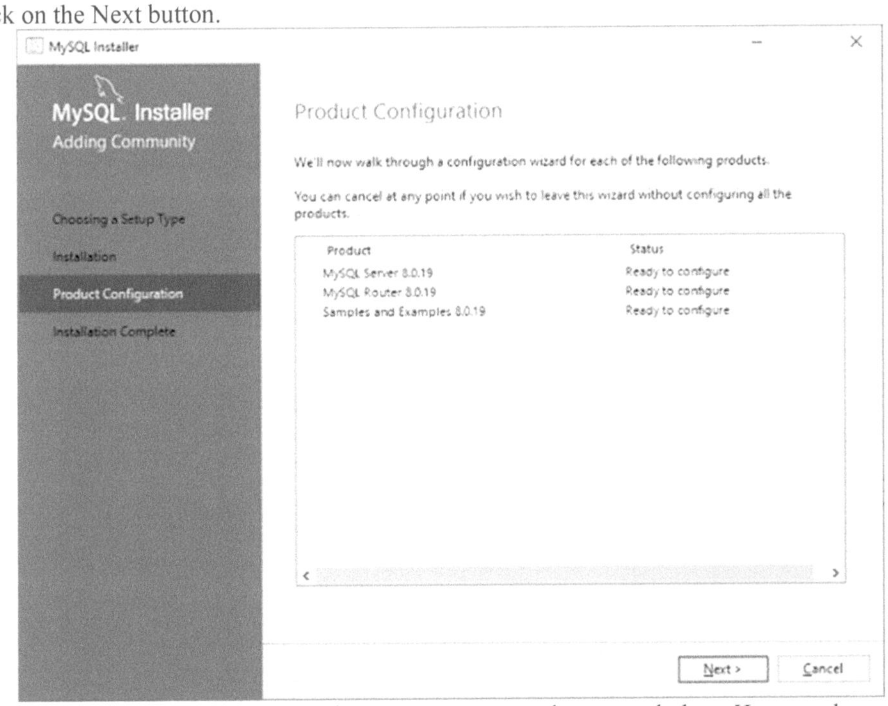

Step 7: As soon as you will click on the Next button, you can see the screen below. Here, we have to configure the MySQL Server. Now, choose the Standalone MySQL Server/Classic MySQL Replication option and click on Next. Here, you can also choose the InnoDB Cluster based on your needs.

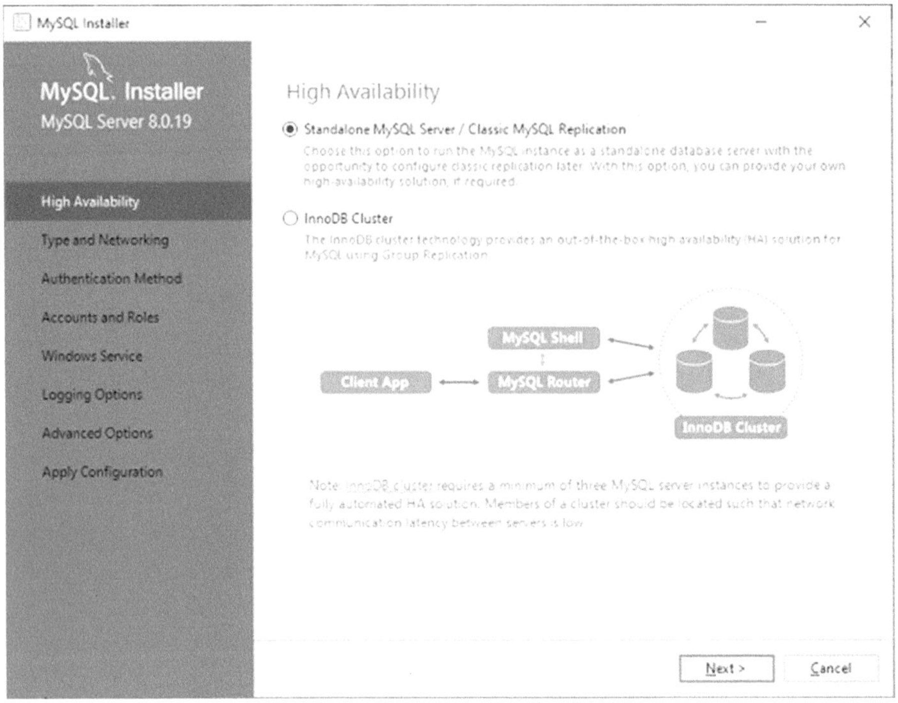

Step 8: In the next screen, the system will ask you to choose the Config Type and other connectivity options. Here, we are going to select the **Config Type** as 'Development Machine' and Connectivity as **TCP/IP,** and **Port Number** is 3306, then click on Next.

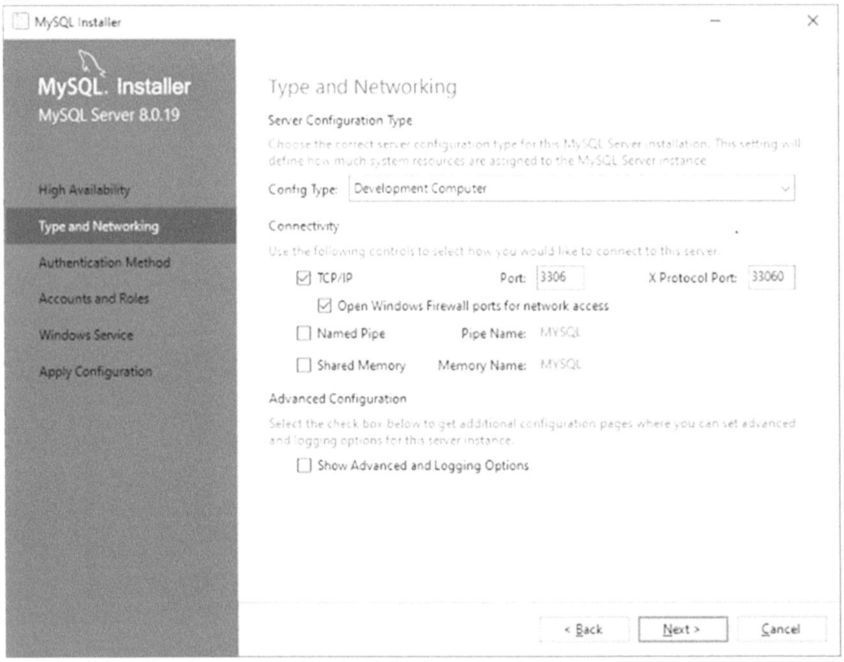

Step 9: Now, select the Authentication Method and click on Next. Here, I am going to select the first option.

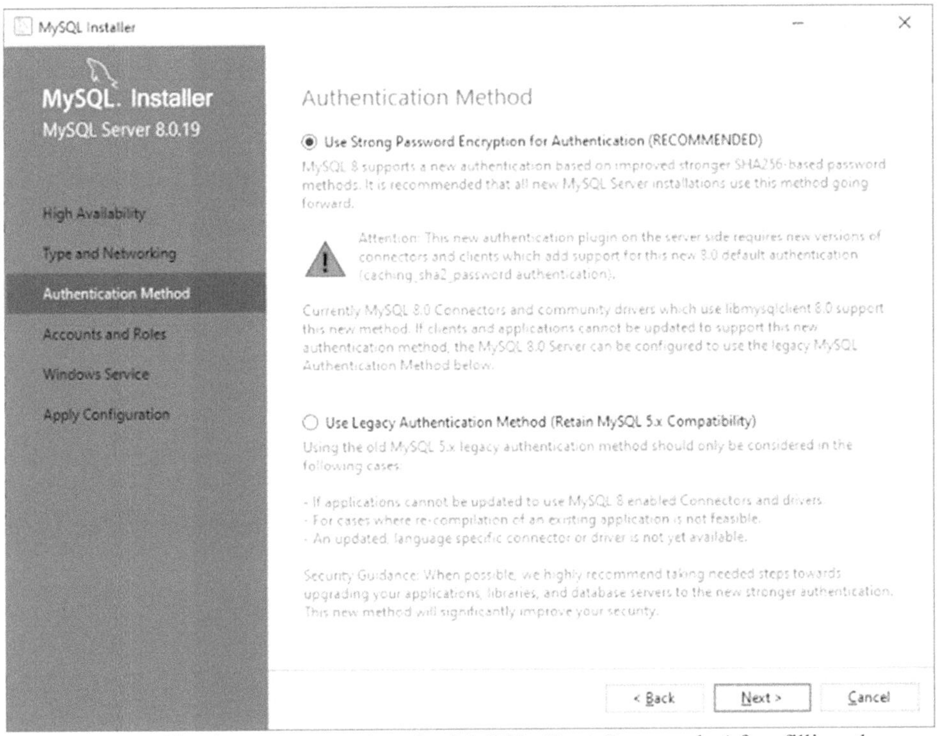

Step 10: The next screen will ask you to mention the MySQL Root Password. After filling the password details, click on the Next button.

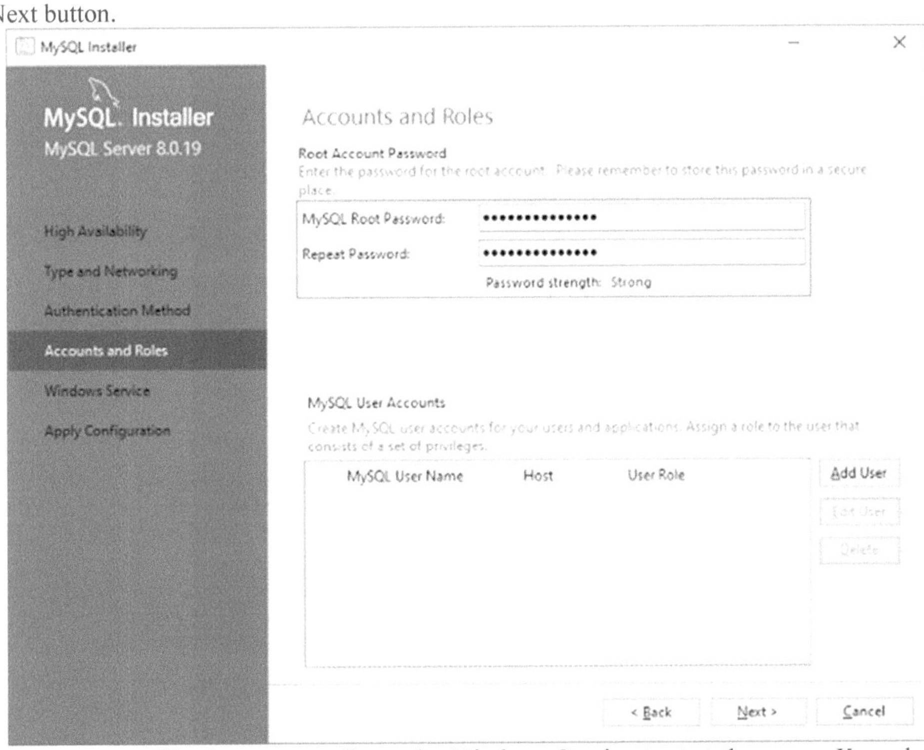

Step 11: The next screen will ask you to configure the Windows Service to start the server. Keep the default setup and click on the Next button.

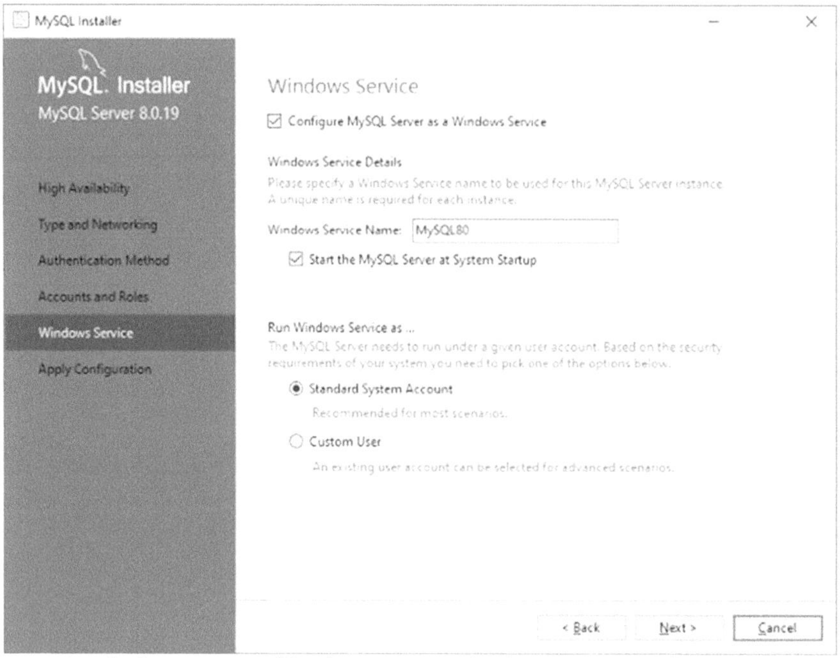

Step 12: In the next wizard, the system will ask you to apply the Server Configuration. If you agree with this configuration, click on the Execute button.

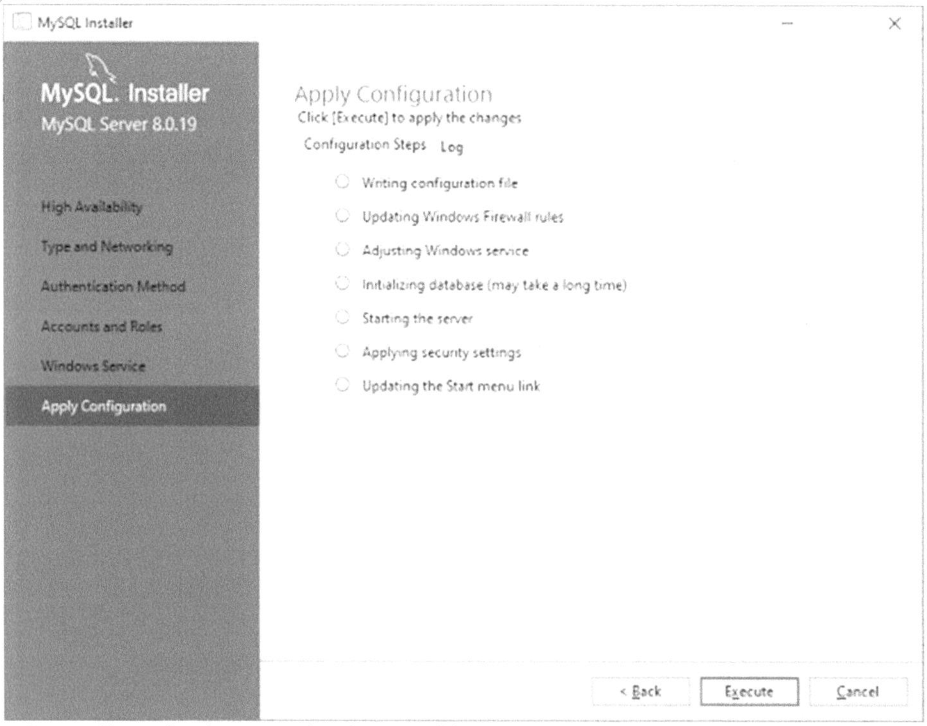

Step 13: Once the configuration has completed, you will get the screen below. Now, click on the **Finish** button to continue.

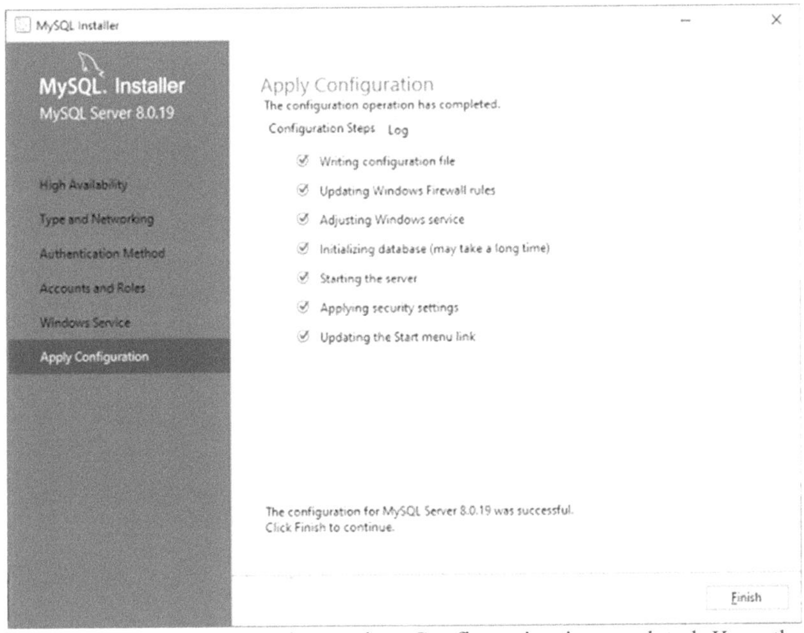

Step 14: In the next screen, you can see that the Product Configuration is completed. Keep the default setting and click on the Next-> Finish button to complete the MySQL package installation.

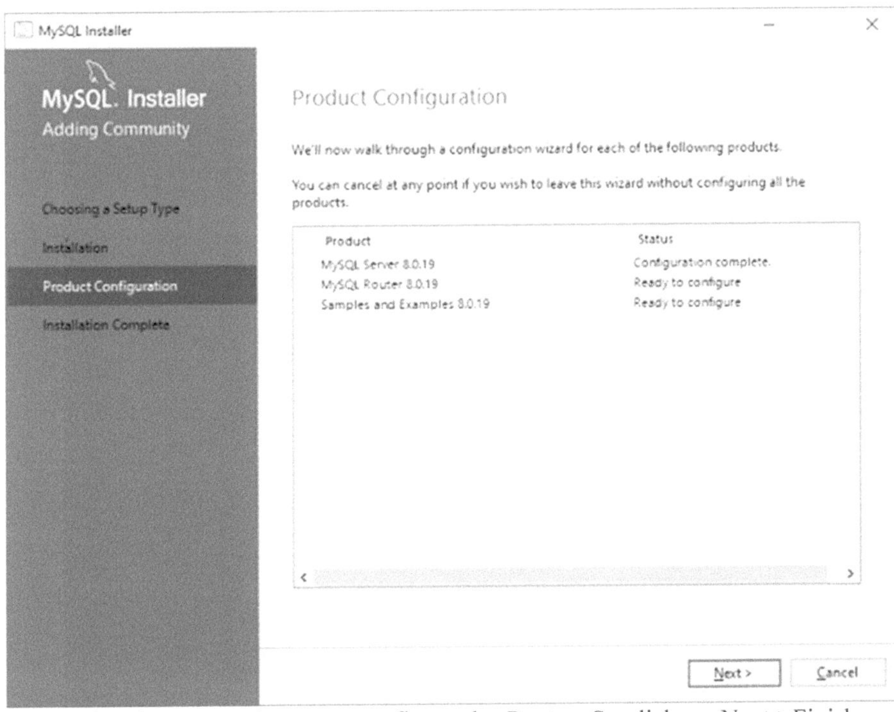

Step 15: In the next wizard, we can choose to configure the Router. So click on Next->Finish and then click the Next button.

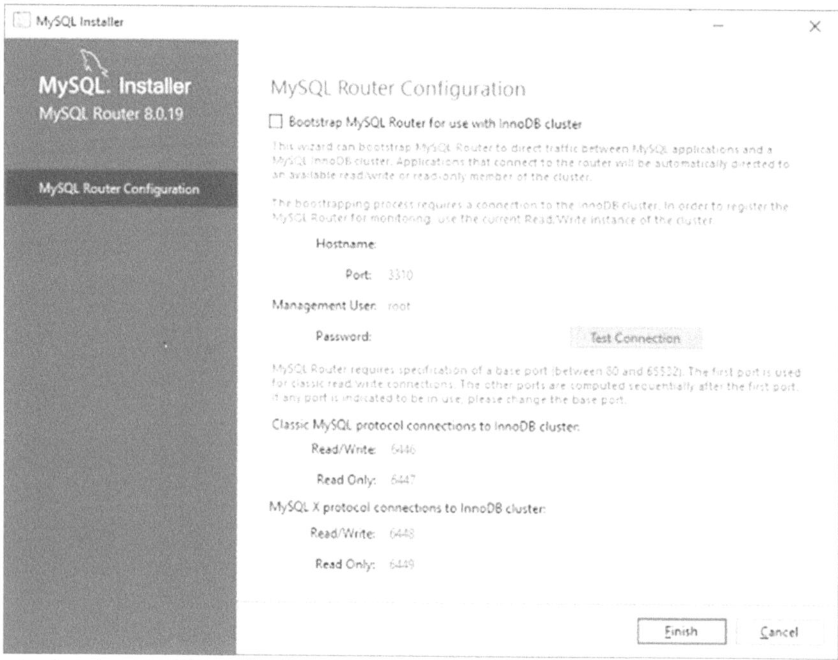

Step 16: In the next wizard, we will see the Connect to Server option. Here, we have to mention the root password, which we had set in the previous steps.

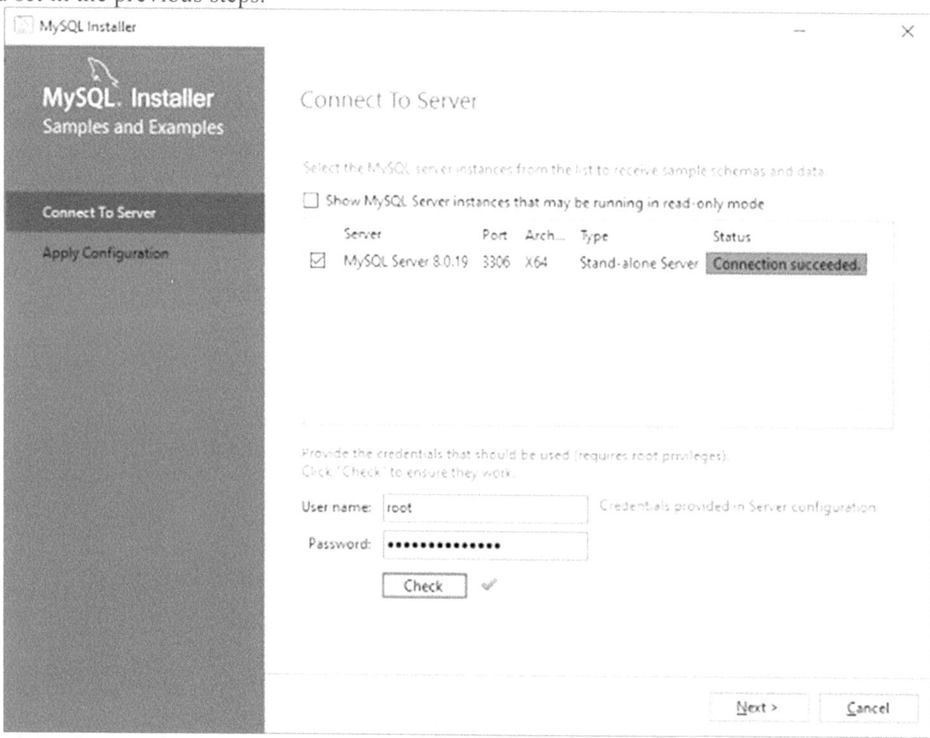

In this screen, it is also required to check about the connection is successful or not by clicking on the Check button. If the connection is successful, click on the Execute button. Now, the configuration is complete, click on Next.

Step 17: In the next wizard, select the applied configurations and click on the Execute button.

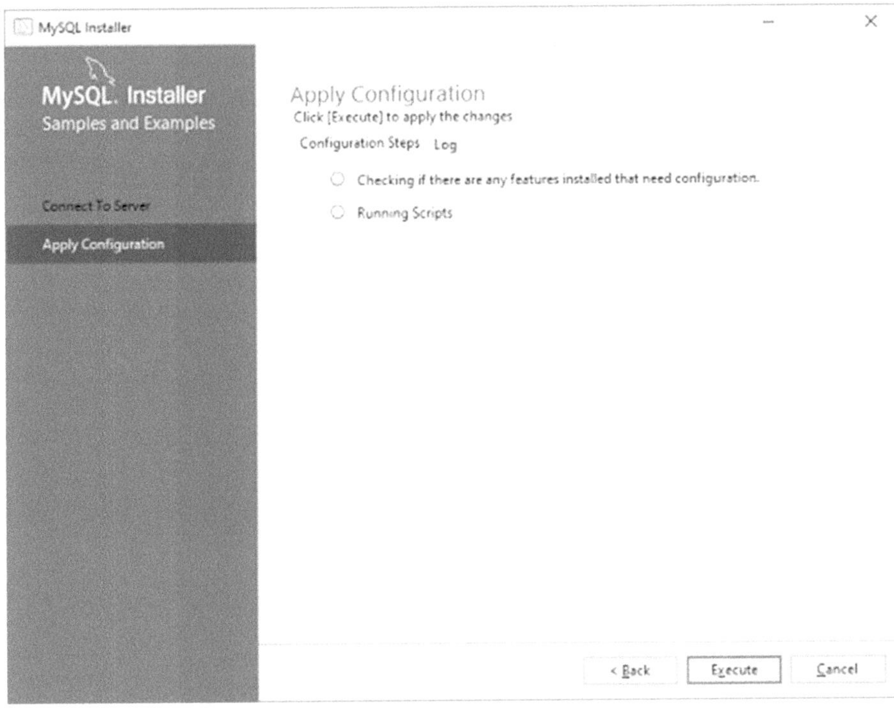

Step 18: After completing the above step, we will get the following screen. Here, click on the Finish button.

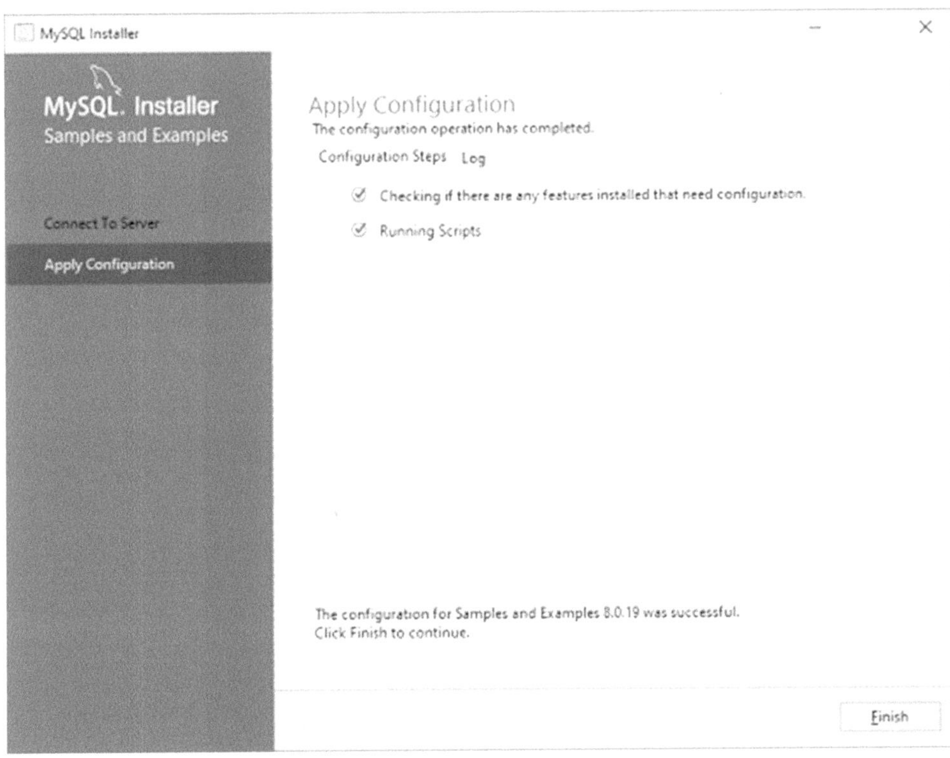

Step 19: Now, the MySQL installation is complete. Click on the Finish button.

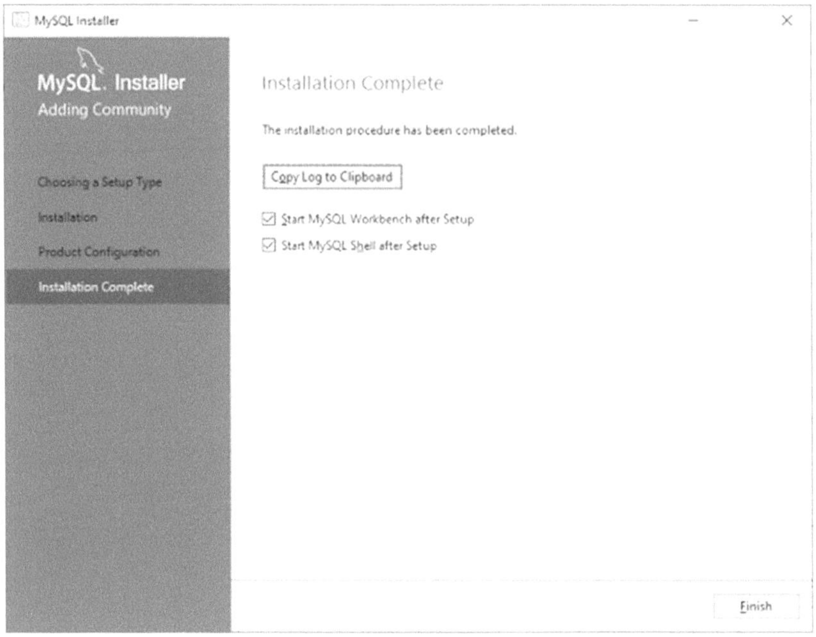

Online Resources:

How to Install MySQL: https://youtu.be/drGz7of1xHQ

QR Code:

MySQL: Quick Introduction: https://youtu.be/-7NOhrJoDko

QR Code:

Database Management System Introduction: https://youtu.be/SwB6RTAQ-o0

QR Code:

Chapter 2: MySQL Basics

Study and Implementation of
MySQL Data Types
Creating Databases and Tables
Inserting Data into Tables
Retrieving Data using SELECT Queries
Updating and Deleting Data

Objective:
Explore the concept of tables, rows, columns, and relationships within a database.
Construct and execute simple SELECT queries to retrieve specific data from tables.
Practice using WHERE clauses, ORDER BY, and GROUP BY to filter, sort, and aggregate retrieved data.

LAB PRACTICE ASSIGNMENT:

Create a table employee_details with columns representing different data types such as INTEGER, VARCHAR, DATE, and DECIMAL.

Solution:

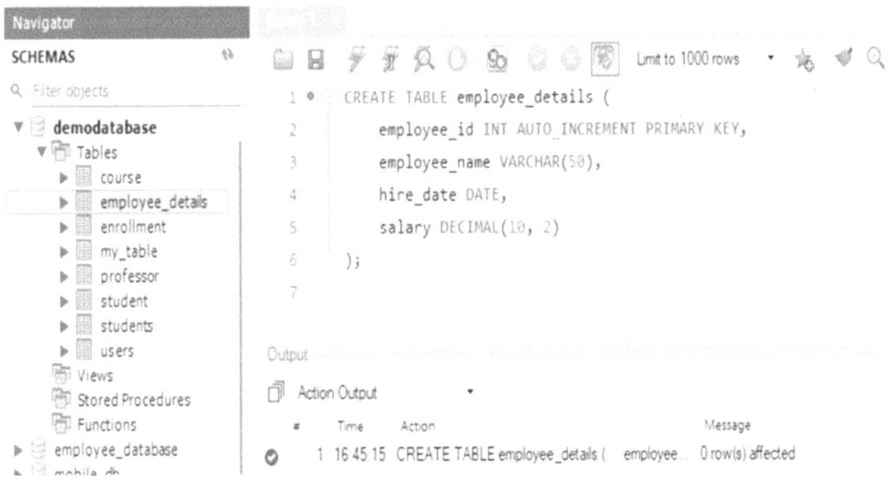

This SQL script creates a table **employee_details** with columns:
employee_id of type INTEGER (INT).
employee_name of type VARCHAR with a maximum length of 50 characters.
hire_date of type DATE to store date values.
salary of type DECIMAL(10, 2) for storing decimal numbers with a total of 10 digits, 2 of which are after the decimal point.

Insert sample data into this table, ensuring you cover various data types.

Solution:

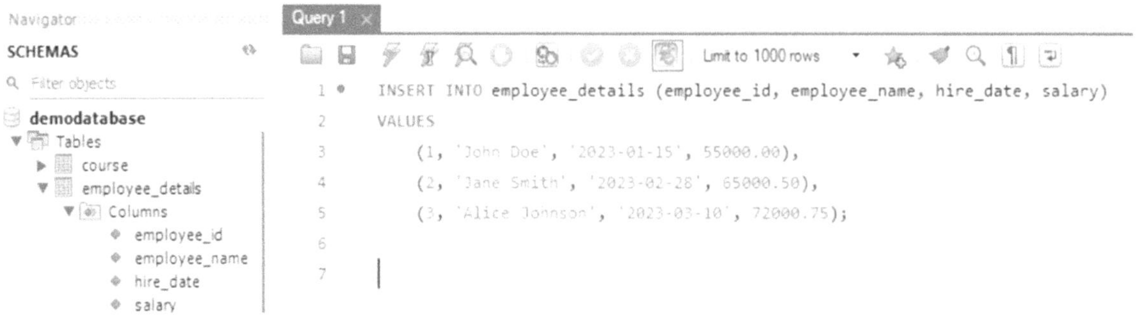

This SQL script inserts three rows of sample data into the **employee_details** table:
employee_id values are integers.
employee_name values are strings (VARCHAR).
hire_date values are in the 'YYYY-MM-DD' format (DATE data type).
salary values are decimal numbers (DECIMAL).

Retrieve and display the inserted data to verify the correct storage and retrieval of different data types.

Solution:

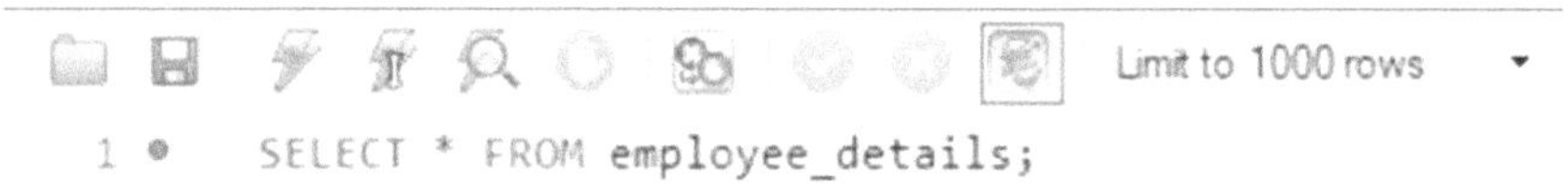

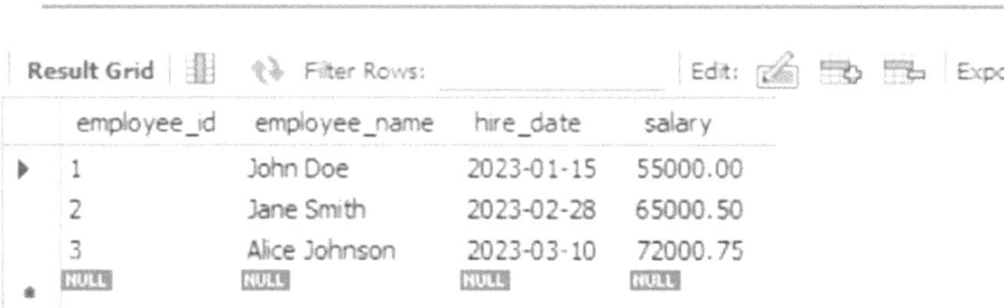

Running this SQL query will retrieve all columns and rows from the **employee_details** table and display them. This will verify the correctness of the storage and retrieval of different data types within the table.

Create a new database named company_db.

Solution:

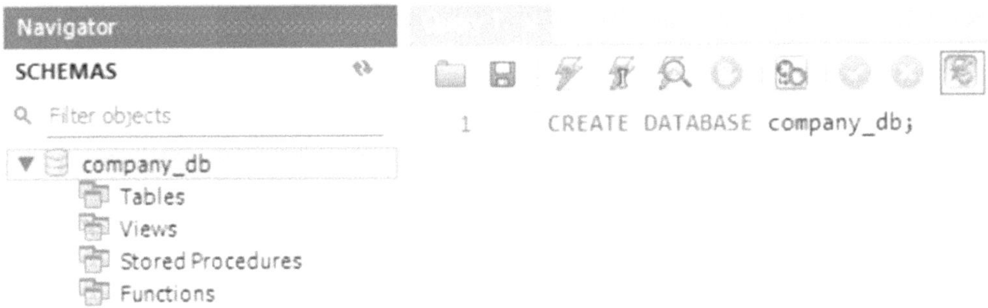

Within this database, create a table named employees with columns like id (INT), name (VARCHAR), designation (VARCHAR), and joining_date (DATE).

Solution:

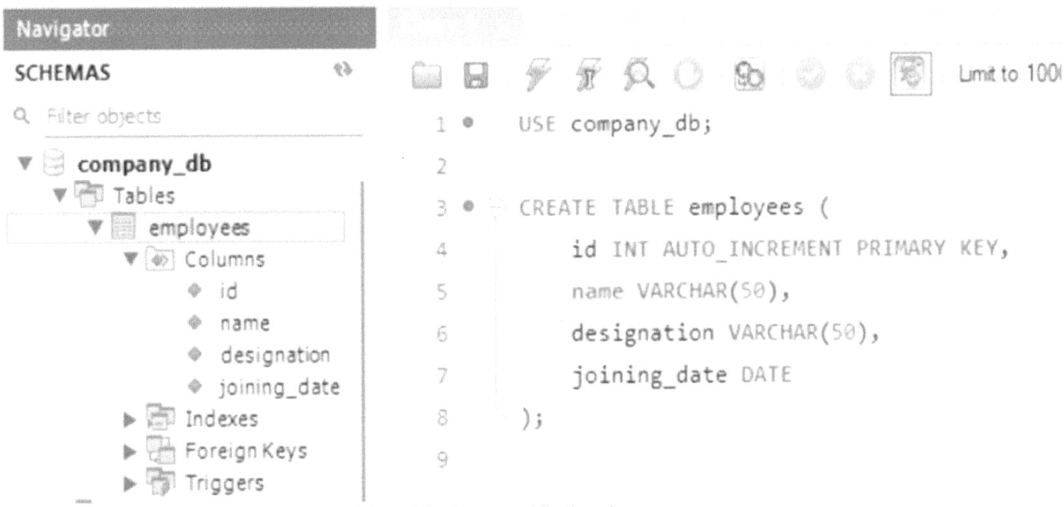

This SQL script creates the **employees** table with the specified columns:
id as an INTEGER (INT) type, set as the primary key with AUTO_INCREMENT for automatic numbering.
name as a VARCHAR with a maximum length of 50 characters.
designation as a VARCHAR with a maximum length of 50 characters.
joining_date as a DATE type to store date values.

Ensure appropriate data types, constraints, and relationships (if needed) are set during table creation.

Solution:

```
USE company_db;

CREATE TABLE employees (
id INT AUTO_INCREMENT PRIMARY KEY,
name VARCHAR(100) NOT NULL,
designation VARCHAR(50),
joining_date DATE,
CONSTRAINT unique_name UNIQUE (name)
);
```

Explanation:

id is set as the primary key with AUTO_INCREMENT to generate unique IDs automatically.
name is set as VARCHAR(100) and specified as NOT NULL to ensure all entries have a name. Additionally, a UNIQUE constraint is added to ensure each name is unique.
designation is set as VARCHAR(50) to hold job titles or roles.
joining_date is set as DATE to store the date an employee joined

Insert several records into the employees table within the company_db database, covering various roles, names, and joining dates.

Solution:

```sql
USE company_db;

INSERT INTO employees (name, designation, joining_date)
VALUES
    ('John Doe', 'Manager', '2022-05-10'),
    ('Jane Smith', 'Developer', '2023-01-15'),
    ('Alice Johnson', 'HR Specialist', '2023-03-28'),
    ('Bob Anderson', 'Sales Executive', '2023-02-05'),
    ('Eva Wilson', 'Marketing Coordinator', '2022-11-20');
```

Include diverse data, ensuring different data types are utilized, such as strings, numbers, and dates.

Solution:

```sql
USE company_db;

INSERT INTO employees (name, designation, joining_date)
VALUES
    ('John Doe', 'Manager', '2022-05-15'),
    ('Jane Smith', 'Developer', '2023-01-10'),
    ('Alice Johnson', 'HR Specialist', '2023-03-20'),
    ('Bob Anderson', 'Marketing Coordinator', '2022-11-05'),
    ('Michael Brown', 'Engineer', '2022-09-30'),
    ('Susan Miller', 'Analyst', '2022-12-25'),
    ('David Wilson', 'Sales Representative', '2023-02-28');
```

Verify successful insertion by querying the table and displaying the inserted data.

Solution:

To verify the successful insertion of data into the **employees** table within the **company_db** database, you can execute a SELECT query to display the inserted data:

```sql
USE company_db;

SELECT * FROM employees;
```

id	name	designation	joining_date
1	John Doe	Manager	2022-05-10
2	Jane Smith	Developer	2023-01-15
3	Alice Johnson	HR Specialist	2023-03-28
4	Bob Anderson	Sales Executive	2023-02-05
5	Eva Wilson	Marketing Coordinator	2022-11-20
6	John Doe	Manager	2022-05-15
7	Jane Smith	Developer	2023-01-10
8	Alice Johnson	HR Specialist	2023-03-20
9	Bob Anderson	Marketing Coordinator	2022-11-05
10	Michael Brown	Engineer	2022-09-30
11	Susan Miller	Analyst	2022-12-25
12	David Wilson	Sales Representative	2023-02-28
NULL	NULL	NULL	NULL

Use SELECT queries to retrieve different subsets of data from the employees table.

Solution:

SELECT queries to retrieve different subsets of data from the **employees** table within the **company_db** database:

Selecting All Columns:

Retrieve all columns and rows from the **employees** table:


```sql
USE company_db;

SELECT * FROM employees;
```

id	name	designation	joining_date
1	John Doe	Manager	2022-05-10
2	Jane Smith	Developer	2023-01-15
3	Alice Johnson	HR Specialist	2023-03-28
4	Bob Anderson	Sales Executive	2023-02-05
5	Eva Wilson	Marketing Coordinator	2022-11-20
6	John Doe	Manager	2022-05-15
7	Jane Smith	Developer	2023-01-10
8	Alice Johnson	HR Specialist	2023-03-20
9	Bob Anderson	Marketing Coordinator	2022-11-05
10	Michael Brown	Engineer	2022-09-30
11	Susan Miller	Analyst	2022-12-25
12	David Wilson	Sales Representative	2023-02-28
NULL	NULL	NULL	NULL

Selecting Specific Columns:
Retrieve specific columns (e.g., name and designation) from the **employees** table:

Limit to 1000 rows

```sql
SELECT name, designation FROM employees;
```

Result Grid | Filter Rows: | Export: | Wrap Cell

name	designation
John Doe	Manager
Jane Smith	Developer
Alice Johnson	HR Specialist
Bob Anderson	Sales Executive
Eva Wilson	Marketing Coordinator
John Doe	Manager
Jane Smith	Developer
Alice Johnson	HR Specialist
Bob Anderson	Marketing Coordinator
Michael Brown	Engineer
Susan Miller	Analyst
David Wilson	Sales Representative

Filtering Data with WHERE:
Retrieve specific records based on a condition (e.g., employees who joined after a certain date):

```sql
SELECT * FROM employees WHERE joining_date > '2023-01-01';
```

Result Grid | Filter Rows: | Edit: | Export/Import:

id	name	designation	joining_date
2	Jane Smith	Developer	2023-01-15
3	Alice Johnson	HR Specialist	2023-03-28
4	Bob Anderson	Sales Executive	2023-02-05
7	Jane Smith	Developer	2023-01-10
8	Alice Johnson	HR Specialist	2023-03-20
12	David Wilson	Sales Representative	2023-02-28
NULL	NULL	NULL	NULL

Ordering Data with ORDER BY:
Retrieve data ordered by a specific column (e.g., ordering by name in ascending order):

```
SELECT * FROM employees ORDER BY name ASC;
```

Result Grid | Filter Rows: | Edit:

id	name	designation	joining_date
3	Alice Johnson	HR Specialist	2023-03-28
8	Alice Johnson	HR Specialist	2023-03-20
4	Bob Anderson	Sales Executive	2023-02-05
9	Bob Anderson	Marketing Coordinator	2022-11-05
12	David Wilson	Sales Representative	2023-02-28
5	Eva Wilson	Marketing Coordinator	2022-11-20
2	Jane Smith	Developer	2023-01-15
7	Jane Smith	Developer	2023-01-10
1	John Doe	Manager	2022-05-10
6	John Doe	Manager	2022-05-15
10	Michael Brown	Engineer	2022-09-30
11	Susan Miller	Analyst	2022-12-25
NULL	NULL	NULL	NULL

Limiting Rows with LIMIT:
Retrieve a limited number of rows (e.g., the first three records):

```
SELECT * FROM employees LIMIT 3;
```

Result Grid | Filter Rows: | Edit:

id	name	designation	joining_date
1	John Doe	Manager	2022-05-10
2	Jane Smith	Developer	2023-01-15
3	Alice Johnson	HR Specialist	2023-03-28
NULL	NULL	NULL	NULL

Update the records in the employees table by modifying specific columns for certain employees (e.g., changing their designation or joining date).

Solution:

```sql
USE company_db;

-- Update designation for an employee with id = 3
UPDATE employees
SET designation = 'Senior Developer'
WHERE id = 3;

-- Update joining date for an employee named 'Jane Smith'
UPDATE employees
SET joining_date = '2022-08-25'
WHERE name = 'Jane Smith';
```

Delete one or more records from the table based on specific criteria, such as deleting an employee who has left the company.

Solution:

```sql
USE company_db;

-- Delete an employee who has left based on a specific condition (e.g., resignation date is not null)
DELETE FROM employees
WHERE resignation_date IS NOT NULL;
```

Chapter 3: Select, From and Where

For the Database CompanyDatabase having 2 tables EmployeeInfo and EmployeePosition with the details as below:

EmployeeInfo:
EmpID INT PRIMARY KEY,
EmpFname VARCHAR(50),
EmpLname VARCHAR(50),
Department VARCHAR(50),
Project VARCHAR(50),
Address VARCHAR(100),
DOB DATE,
Gender CHAR(1)

EmployeePosition:
EmpID INT,
EmpPosition VARCHAR(50),
DateOfJoining DATE,
Salary DECIMAL(10, 2)

With the following values:

EmployeeInfo Table:

EmpID	EmpFname	EmpLname	Department	Project	Address	DOB	Gender
1	Sanjay	Mehra	HR	P1	Hyderabad(HYD)	01/12/1976	M
2	Ananya	Mishra	Admin	P2	Delhi(DEL)	02/05/1968	F
3	Rohan	Diwan	Account	P3	Mumbai(BOM)	01/01/1980	M
4	Sonia	Kulkarni	HR	P1	Hyderabad(HYD)	02/05/1992	F
5	Ankit	Kapoor	Admin	P2	Delhi(DEL)	03/07/1994	M

EmployeePosition Table:

EmpID	EmpPosition	DateOfJoining	Salary
1	Manager	01/05/2022	500000
2	Executive	02/05/2022	75000
3	Manager	01/05/2022	90000
2	Lead	02/05/2022	85000
1	Executive	01/05/2022	300000

Perform the following Select, From, Where Statement:
Retrieve Employee Names and Departments:
Get Employee Names, Positions, and Salaries:
List Employees in HR Department
Find Employees in Hyderabad
Retrieve Employee Names, Positions, and Joining Dates

Solution:

Retrieve Employee Names and Departments:

```sql
SELECT EmpFname, EmpLname, Department
FROM EmployeeInfo;
```

100 %

Results | Messages

	EmpFname	EmpLname	Department
1	Sanjay	Mehra	HR
2	Ananya	Mishra	Admin
3	Rohan	Diwan	Account
4	Sonia	Kulkarni	HR
5	Ankit	Kapoor	Admin

Get Employee Names, Positions, and Salaries.

```sql
SELECT EI.EmpFname, EI.EmpLname, EP.EmpPosition, EP.Salary
FROM EmployeeInfo EI
JOIN EmployeePosition EP ON EI.EmpID = EP.EmpID;
```

100 %

Results | Messages

	EmpFname	EmpLname	EmpPosition	Salary
1	Sanjay	Mehra	Manager	500000.00
2	Ananya	Mishra	Executive	75000.00
3	Rohan	Diwan	Manager	90000.00
4	Ananya	Mishra	Lead	85000.00
5	Sanjay	Mehra	Executive	300000.00

List Employees in HR Department

```sql
SELECT *
FROM EmployeeInfo
WHERE Department = 'HR';
```

100 %

Results | Messages

	EmpID	EmpFname	EmpLname	Department	Project	Address	DOB	Gender
1	1	Sanjay	Mehra	HR	P1	Hyderabad (HYD)	1976-12-01	M
2	4	Sonia	Kulkarni	HR	P1	Hyderabad (HYD)	1992-05-02	F

Find Employees in Hyderabad

```sql
SELECT *
FROM EmployeeInfo
WHERE Address LIKE '%Hyderabad%';
```

100 %

Results | Messages

	EmpID	EmpFname	EmpLname	Department	Project	Address	DOB	Gender
1	1	Sanjay	Mehra	HR	P1	Hyderabad (HYD)	1976-12-01	M
2	4	Sonia	Kulkarni	HR	P1	Hyderabad (HYD)	1992-05-02	F

Retrieve Employee Names, Positions, and Joining Dates

```sql
SELECT EI.EmpFname, EI.EmpLname, EP.EmpPosition, EP.DateOfJoining
FROM EmployeeInfo EI
JOIN EmployeePosition EP ON EI.EmpID = EP.EmpID;
```

100 %

Results | Messages

	EmpFname	EmpLname	EmpPosition	DateOfJoining
1	Sanjay	Mehra	Manager	2022-05-01
2	Ananya	Mishra	Executive	2022-05-02
3	Rohan	Diwan	Manager	2022-05-01
4	Ananya	Mishra	Lead	2022-05-02
5	Sanjay	Mehra	Executive	2022-05-01

Practice Questions

List Employee Names and Salaries:

```sql
SELECT EmpFname, EmpLname, Salary
FROM EmployeeInfo EI
JOIN EmployeePosition EP ON EI.EmpID = EP.EmpID;
```

Results | Messages

	EmpFname	EmpLname	Salary
1	Sanjay	Mehra	500000.00
2	Ananya	Mishra	75000.00
3	Rohan	Diwan	90000.00
4	Ananya	Mishra	85000.00
5	Sanjay	Mehra	300000.00

Count Employees in Each Department:

```sql
SELECT Department, COUNT(*) AS EmployeeCount
FROM EmployeeInfo
GROUP BY Department;
```

100 %

Results | Messages

	Department	EmployeeCount
1	Account	1
2	Admin	2
3	HR	2

Calculate Average Salary of Managers:

```sql
SELECT AVG(Salary) AS AvgManagerSalary
FROM EmployeePosition
WHERE EmpPosition = 'Manager';
```

100 %

Results | Messages

	AvgManagerSalary
1	295000.000000

Find the Highest Salary:

```sql
SELECT MAX(Salary) AS MaxSalary
FROM EmployeePosition;
```

100 %

Results | Messages

	MaxSalary
1	500000.00

List Employees Older Than 40:

```sql
SELECT EmpFname, EmpLname, DATEADD(year, 40, DOB) AS DateAfter40
FROM EmployeeInfo
WHERE DOB < DATEADD(year, -40, GETDATE());
```

100 %

Results Messages

	EmpFname	EmpLname	DateAfter40
1	Sanjay	Mehra	2016-12-01
2	Ananya	Mishra	2008-05-02
3	Rohan	Diwan	2020-01-01

Retrieve Employee Names in HR Department:

```sql
SELECT EmpFname, EmpLname
FROM EmployeeInfo
WHERE EmpID IN (SELECT EmpID FROM EmployeePosition WHERE EmpPosition = 'HR');
```

100 %

Results Messages

EmpFname	EmpLname

Find the Lowest Salary Among Executives:

```sql
SELECT MIN(Salary) AS MinSalary
FROM EmployeePosition
WHERE EmpPosition = 'Executive';
```

100 %

Results Messages

	MinSalary
1	75000.00

List Employees in Hyderabad Working on Project P1:

```
SELECT EmpFname, EmpLname
FROM EmployeeInfo
WHERE EmpID IN (
    SELECT EP.EmpID
    FROM EmployeePosition EP
    JOIN EmployeeInfo EI ON EP.EmpID = EI.EmpID
    WHERE Address = 'Hyderabad(HYD)' AND Project = 'P1'
);
```

.00 %

Results   Messages

EmpFname	EmpLname

Count Employees with a Salary Greater Than Average:

```
SELECT COUNT(*) AS AboveAvgSalaryCount
FROM EmployeePosition
WHERE Salary > (
    SELECT AVG(Salary) AS AvgSalary
    FROM EmployeePosition
);
```

100 %

Results   Messages

	AboveAvgSalaryCount
1	2

Find Employees Who Joined Before Their Managers:

```sql
SELECT EmpFname, EmpLname
FROM EmployeeInfo
WHERE EmpID IN (
    SELECT EP.EmpID
    FROM EmployeePosition EP
    JOIN EmployeeInfo EI ON EP.EmpID = EI.EmpID
    WHERE EP.DateOfJoining < (
        SELECT EP2.DateOfJoining
        FROM EmployeePosition EP2
        WHERE EP2.EmpPosition = 'Manager' AND EP2.EmpID = EP.EmpID
    )
);
```

100 %

Results Messages

EmpFname	EmpLname

Chapter 4: SQL Queries

Study and Implementation of
Filtering Data with WHERE Clause
Sorting Results with ORDER BY
Aggregate Functions and Grouping Data
Joining Tables
Subqueriesand Nested Queries

Objective:
Understand the usage of the WHERE, ORDER BY, aggregate functions (COUNT, SUM, AVG, MIN, MAX), joins, subqueries and nested queries.
Implement ORDER BY in SELECT queries to organize data output in a specified sequence for improved readability or analysis.
Utilize GROUP BY clauses to categorize data based on specific columns and perform aggregate functions on grouped data sets.
Implement subqueries within SELECT statements to retrieve data based on conditions derived from the results of another query.
Implement join operations to retrieve data from related tables, demonstrating how to link and extract information from connected datasets.

LAB PRACTICE ASSIGNMENT:

Create the database Company.

CREATE DATABASE IF NOT EXISTS Company;

Create table Employee having columns id, name, department, and salary.

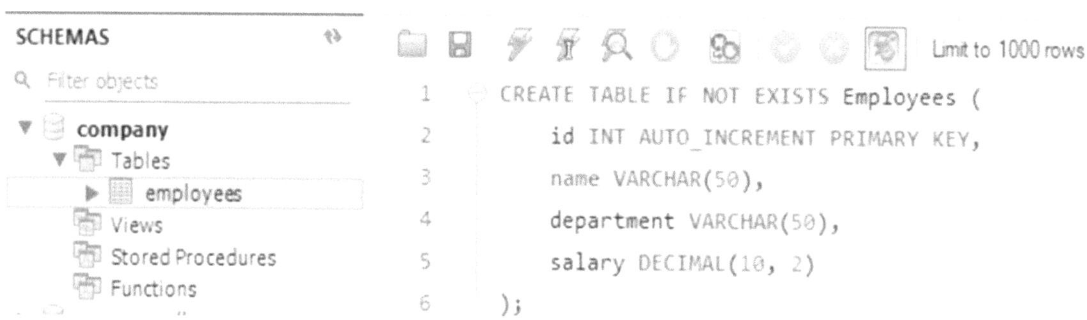

Add Values in the table Employee

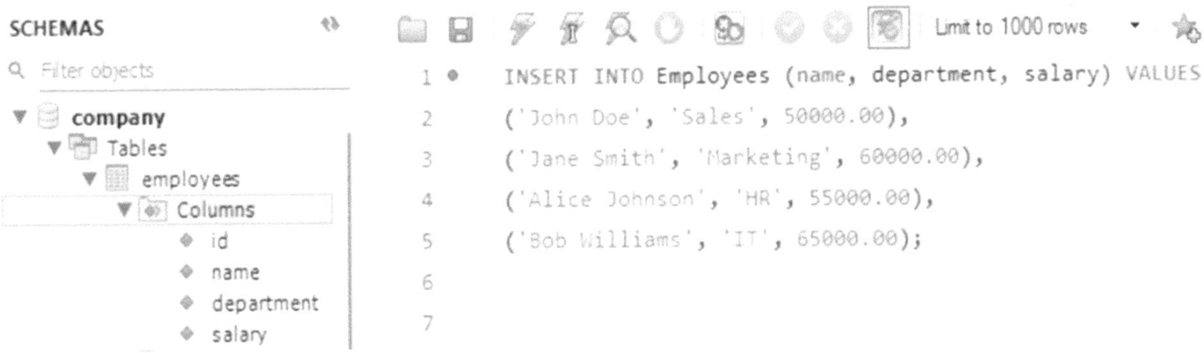

Retrieve employees earning more than $55,000

SELECT * FROM Employees WHERE salary > 55000;

Result Grid | Filter Rows: | Edit:

id	name	department	salary
2	Jane Smith	Marketing	60000.00
4	Bob Williams	IT	65000.00
NULL	NULL	NULL	NULL

Fetch employees from the IT department

SELECT * FROM Employees WHERE department = 'IT';

Result Grid | Filter Rows: | Edit:

id	name	department	salary
4	Bob Williams	IT	65000.00
NULL	NULL	NULL	NULL

Display employee details whose name starts with 'J'

SELECT * FROM Employees WHERE name LIKE 'J%';

Result Grid | Filter Rows:

id	name	department	salary
1	John Doe	Sales	50000.00
2	Jane Smith	Marketing	60000.00
NULL	NULL	NULL	NULL

Get employees whose salary is between $50,000 and $60,000

SELECT * FROM Employees WHERE salary BETWEEN 50000 AND 60000;

	id	name	department	salary
▶	1	John Doe	Sales	50000.00
	2	Jane Smith	Marketing	60000.00
	3	Alice Johnson	HR	55000.00
*	NULL	NULL	NULL	NULL

Retrieve employees with 'hn' anywhere in their names

SELECT * FROM Employees WHERE name LIKE '%hn%';

	id	name	department	salary
▶	1	John Doe	Sales	50000.00
	3	Alice Johnson	HR	55000.00
*	NULL	NULL	NULL	NULL

Fetch employees earning the maximum salary

SELECT * FROM Employees WHERE salary = (SELECT MAX(salary) FROM Employees);

	id	name	department	salary
▶	4	Bob Williams	IT	65000.00
*	NULL	NULL	NULL	NULL

Display employees except those from the Sales department

SELECT * FROM Employees WHERE department <> 'Sales';

	id	name	department	salary
▶	2	Jane Smith	Marketing	60000.00
	3	Alice Johnson	HR	55000.00
	4	Bob Williams	IT	65000.00
*	NULL	NULL	NULL	NULL

Get employees with an ID greater than 2

SELECT * FROM Employees WHERE id > 2;

id	name	department	salary
3	Alice Johnson	HR	55000.00
4	Bob Williams	IT	65000.00
NULL	NULL	NULL	NULL

Retrieve employees whose names are not 'John Doe'

SELECT * FROM Employees WHERE name! = 'John Doe';

id	name	department	salary
2	Jane Smith	Marketing	60000.00
3	Alice Johnson	HR	55000.00
4	Bob Williams	IT	65000.00
NULL	NULL	NULL	NULL

Fetch employees from the Marketing department with a salary greater than $55,000

SELECT * FROM Employees WHERE department = 'Marketing' AND salary > 55000;

id	name	department	salary
2	Jane Smith	Marketing	60000.00
NULL	NULL	NULL	NULL

Sorting by name in ascending order

SELECT * FROM Employees ORDER BY name ASC;

id	name	department	salary
3	Alice Johnson	HR	55000.00
4	Bob Williams	IT	65000.00
2	Jane Smith	Marketing	60000.00
1	John Doe	Sales	50000.00
NULL	NULL	NULL	NULL

Sorting by department in descending order

SELECT * FROM Employees ORDER BY department DESC;

id	name	department	salary
1	John Doe	Sales	50000.00
2	Jane Smith	Marketing	60000.00
4	Bob Williams	IT	65000.00
3	Alice Johnson	HR	55000.00
NULL	NULL	NULL	NULL

Sorting by salary in descending order

SELECT * FROM Employees ORDER BY salary DESC;

id	name	department	salary
4	Bob Williams	IT	65000.00
2	Jane Smith	Marketing	60000.00
3	Alice Johnson	HR	55000.00
1	John Doe	Sales	50000.00
NULL	NULL	NULL	NULL

Sorting by department in ascending order and then by salary in descending order

SELECT * FROM Employees ORDER BY department ASC, salary DESC;

id	name	department	salary
3	Alice Johnson	HR	55000.00
4	Bob Williams	IT	65000.00
2	Jane Smith	Marketing	60000.00
1	John Doe	Sales	50000.00
NULL	NULL	NULL	NULL

Count the number of employees

SELECT COUNT(*) AS TotalEmployees FROM Employees;

TotalEmployees
4

Calculate the total salary of all employees

SELECT SUM(salary) AS TotalSalary FROM Employees;

TotalSalary
230000.00

Find the average salary of employees

```
SELECT AVG(salary) AS AvgSalary FROM Employees;
```

AvgSalary
57500.000000

Find the maximum salary among employees

```
SELECT MAX(salary) AS MaxSalary FROM Employees;
```

MaxSalary
65000.00

Find the minimum salary among employees

```
SELECT MIN(salary) AS MinSalary FROM Employees;
```

MinSalary
50000.00

Count employees in each department

```
SELECT department, COUNT(*) AS EmployeeCount
FROM Employees
GROUP BY department;
```

department	EmployeeCount
Sales	1
Marketing	1
HR	1
IT	1

Calculate average salary by department

```
SELECT department, AVG(salary) AS AvgSalary
FROM Employees
GROUP BY department;
```

department	AvgSalary
Sales	50000.000000
Marketing	60000.000000
HR	55000.000000
IT	65000.000000

Find count and average salary by department

```
SELECT department, COUNT(*) AS EmployeeCount, AVG(salary) AS AvgSalary
FROM Employees
GROUP BY department;
```

department	EmployeeCount	AvgSalary
Sales	1	50000.000000
Marketing	1	60000.000000
HR	1	55000.000000
IT	1	65000.000000

Retrieve Employees with Salaries Higher than the Average:

```
SELECT * FROM Employees WHERE salary > (SELECT AVG(salary) FROM Employees);
```

Result Grid | Filter Rows:

id	name	department	salary
2	Jane Smith	Marketing	60000.00
4	Bob Williams	IT	65000.00
NULL	NULL	NULL	NULL

Fetch Employees from the Marketing Department with Higher Salary than the Average in IT:

```
SELECT * FROM Employees
WHERE department = 'Marketing'
AND salary > (SELECT AVG(salary) FROM Employees WHERE department = 'IT');
```

Result Grid | Filter Rows:

id	name	department	salary
NULL	NULL	NULL	NULL

Using a Nested Query to Get Employees from the Sales Department:

```
SELECT * FROM Employees
WHERE department = (SELECT department FROM Employees WHERE name = 'John Doe');
```

Result Grid | Filter Rows:

id	name	department	salary
1	John Doe	Sales	50000.00
NULL	NULL	NULL	NULL

Nested Query for Employees with the Highest Salary:

```
SELECT * FROM Employees
WHERE salary = (SELECT MAX(salary) FROM Employees);
```

Result Grid | Filter Rows:

id	name	department	salary
4	Bob Williams	IT	65000.00
NULL	NULL	NULL	NULL

Chapter 5 : Indexes and Optimization

Study and Implementation of
Understanding Indexes
Creating and Managing Indexes
Query Optimization Techniques

Objective:
Learn the process of creating indexes on specific columns to optimize query performance.
Understand methods to manage, modify, or drop indexes, considering scenarios where index alterations can improve or impact database performance.
Explore optimization techniques like query restructuring, proper indexing, and query caching to enhance query execution speed and efficiency.
Learn methods to evaluate query performance using tools or query analysis, and implement optimizations to achieve faster query response times.

LAB PRACTICE ASSIGNMENT:

Create the table Project in Company databasewith columns project_id, project_name, start_date, and end_date.

Switch to the Company database
USE Company;

Create the Projects table
CREATE TABLE IF NOT EXISTS Projects (
project_id INT AUTO_INCREMENT PRIMARY KEY,
project_name VARCHAR(50),
start_date DATE,
end_date DATE
);

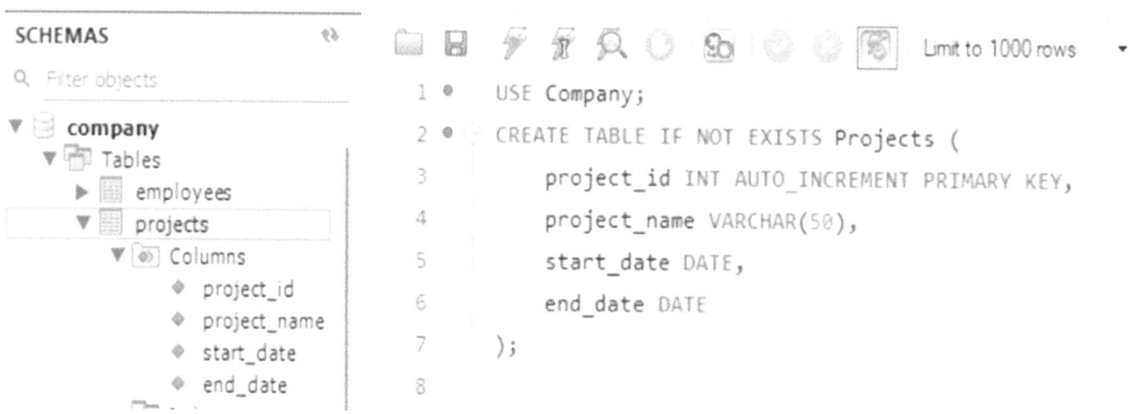

Create indexes on the start_date and end_date columns for efficient querying.
Create an index on start_date column
CREATE INDEX idx_start_date ON Projects(start_date);

Create an index on end_date column
CREATE INDEX idx_end_date ON Projects(end_date);

Manage indexes by adding, dropping, or listing them.
List all indexes on the Projects table
SHOW INDEX FROM Projects;
Drop the index on start_date column
DROP INDEX idx_start_date ON Projects;

Drop the index on end_date column
DROP INDEX idx_end_date ON Projects;

Query using index on start_date column
SELECT * FROM Projects WHERE start_date >= '2023-01-01';

project_id	project_name	start_date	end_date
1	Project Alpha	2023-01-01	2023-06-30
2	Project Beta	2023-02-15	2023-09-30
3	Project Gamma	2023-03-20	2023-08-15
4	Project Delta	2023-04-10	2023-11-30
NULL	NULL	NULL	NULL

Retrieve only necessary columns instead of using SELECT * to reduce data retrieval overhead.

SELECT project_name, start_date FROM Projects WHERE end_date < '2024-01-01';

project_name	start_date
Project Alpha	2023-01-01
Project Gamma	2023-03-20
Project Beta	2023-02-15
Project Delta	2023-04-10

Use appropriate join types (INNER JOIN, LEFT JOIN, etc.) and conditions to prevent unnecessary data retrieval or incorrect results.

Example of INNER JOIN

```
SELECT p.project_name, e.name
FROM Projects p
INNER JOIN Employees e ON p.project_id = e.project_id;
```

project_name	name
Project Alpha	John Doe
Project Alpha	Jane Smith
Project Beta	Alice Johnson
Project Gamma	Bob Williams

Fetch top 2 rows

SELECT * FROM Projects LIMIT 2;

Result Grid | Filter Rows: | Edit:

project_id	project_name	start_date	end_date
1	Project Alpha	2023-01-01	2023-06-30
2	Project Beta	2023-02-15	2023-09-30
NULL	NULL	NULL	NULL

Subquery optimization example

```
SELECT project_id
FROM Projects
WHERE project_id NOT IN (SELECT project_id FROM Employees);
```

Result Grid | Filter Rows:

project_id
4
NULL

Analyse query execution plan

```
EXPLAIN SELECT * FROM Projects WHERE start_date >= '2023-01-01';
```

Result Grid | Filter Rows: | Export: | Wrap Cell Content:

id	select_type	table	partitions	type	possible_keys	key	key_len	ref	rows	filtered	Extra
1	SIMPLE	Projects	NULL	range	idx_start_date	idx_start_date	4	NULL	4	100.00	Using index condition

Chapter 6: Data Manipulation

Study and Implementation of
Transactions and ACID Properties
Working with Views
Stored Procedures and Functions
Triggers and Events

Objective:
Explore the concept of transactions by initiating multiple SQL statements as a single unit of work, ensuring all-or-nothing execution.
Study and demonstrate the four ACID properties (Atomicity, Consistency, Isolation, Durability)
Explore how Views can control data access by limiting columns or rows exposed to users.
Understand the creation and usage of functions to perform specific tasks, enhancing query capabilities and code modularity.
Learn to create triggers that automatically respond to predefined database events (like INSERT, UPDATE, DELETE), executing SQL code accordingly.

LAB PRACTICE ASSIGNMENT:

Define a scenario involving a banking system. Initiate a transaction that transfers funds between two accounts, ensuring either both debiting and crediting occur or neither occurs.

Solution:
Let's simulate a banking scenario where a transaction involves transferring funds between two accounts while ensuring the atomicity, consistency, isolation, and durability (ACID properties) of the transaction.
Consider two hypothetical tables: **Accounts** and **Transactions**.
Accounts Table Schema:

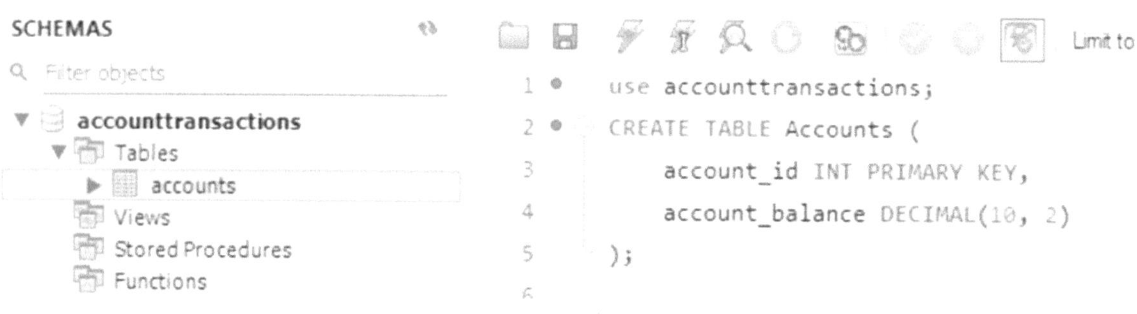

Transactions Table Schema:

Navigator

SCHEMAS

- accounttransactions
  - Tables
    - accounts
    - transactions
  - Views
  - Stored Procedures
  - Functions
- company
- company_db

```sql
use accounttransactions;
CREATE TABLE Transactions (
    transaction_id INT AUTO_INCREMENT PRIMARY KEY,
    from_account_id INT,
    to_account_id INT,
    amount DECIMAL(10, 2),
    transaction_status ENUM('pending', 'completed', 'failed')
);
```

Sample Values for Accounts Table:
Assuming we have two accounts with IDs **123** and **456**:

```sql
INSERT INTO Accounts (account_id, account_balance) VALUES
(123, 1000.00), -- Initial balance for Account ID 123
(456, 500.00);  -- Initial balance for Account ID 456
```

Result Grid

account_id	account_balance
123	1000.00
456	500.00
NULL	NULL

Scenario:
Start Transaction:

```sql
START TRANSACTION;

SELECT * FROM Accounts WHERE account_id = 123 FOR UPDATE;
SELECT * FROM Accounts WHERE account_id = 456 FOR UPDATE;

UPDATE Accounts SET account_balance = account_balance - 100 WHERE account_id = 123;
UPDATE Accounts SET account_balance = account_balance + 100 WHERE account_id = 456;

INSERT INTO Transactions (from_account_id, to_account_id, amount, transaction_status)
VALUES (123, 456, 100, 'pending');

-- Simulating successful completion
COMMIT;
```

Result Grid

account_id	account_balance
456	500.00
NULL	NULL

Displaying Updated Accounts and Transactions:

Accounts Table:

account_id	account_balance
123	900.00
456	600.00
NULL	NULL

Transactions Table:

transaction_id	from_account_id	to_account_id	amount	transaction_status
1	123	456	100.00	completed
NULL	NULL	NULL	NULL	NULL

These values showcase the updated account balances and the completed transaction after transferring funds from Account ID **123** to Account ID **456** with a transfer amount of **100**. Adjust the values or add error scenarios as needed to simulate different outcomes within the transaction.

Simulate an inventory update scenario where multiple SQL statements need to execute together. Show how the atomicity property ensures either all updates succeed or fail together.

Solution:

let's simulate an inventory update scenario involving multiple SQL statements within a transaction to ensure atomicity. Assume we have an **Inventory** table with product quantities.

Inventory Table Schema:

```
SCHEMAS
accounttransactions
  Tables
    accounts
    inventory
    transactions
```

```sql
CREATE TABLE Inventory (
    product_id INT PRIMARY KEY,
    product_name VARCHAR(50),
    quantity INT
);
```

Scenario:

Suppose we want to update the inventory for two products (**product_id** 101 and 102) simultaneously.

```sql
START TRANSACTION;

-- Retrieve and lock rows for the specified products
SELECT * FROM Inventory WHERE product_id IN (101, 102) FOR UPDATE;

-- Update quantities for the specified products
UPDATE Inventory SET quantity = quantity - 10 WHERE product_id = 101;
UPDATE Inventory SET quantity = quantity + 10 WHERE product_id = 102;

-- Commit or Rollback based on success or failure
COMMIT; -- or ROLLBACK;
```

Commit/Rollback:
If both updates succeed:
The quantity for **product_id** 101 will decrease by 10.
The quantity for **product_id** 102 will increase by 10.
Use **COMMIT** to finalize the transaction.
If any update fails (e.g., insufficient quantity, connection issues):
Rollback the transaction using **ROLLBACK**.
Both products' quantities remain unchanged.
This approach ensures that both updates (decrementing quantity for one product and incrementing for another) occur together as a single atomic operation. If any part of the transaction fails, both updates are rolled back, ensuring the consistency of inventory quantities.
Adjust the product IDs, quantities, and error handling logic according to your inventory system requirements and constraints.

Create a situation where concurrent transactions access and update the same dataset. Illustrate isolation levels to manage interference and demonstrate potential inconsistencies without isolation.

Solution:
Let's simulate a scenario where concurrent transactions access and update the same dataset within the **Inventory** table, showcasing isolation levels to manage interference and the potential inconsistencies that might arise without isolation.
Inventory Table Schema:
Assume we have an **Inventory** table with product quantities:
CREATE TABLE Inventory (
product_id INT PRIMARY KEY,
product_name VARCHAR(50),
quantity INT
);
Scenario:
Suppose two transactions concurrently modify the quantity of a specific product (**product_id = 101**) within the **Inventory** table. One transaction attempts to decrement the quantity by 5, while the other attempts to increment it by 10.
Transaction 1 (Decrement by 5):

```
-- Begin Transaction 1
START TRANSACTION;

-- Set Isolation Level for Transaction 1 (Read Committed)
SET TRANSACTION ISOLATION LEVEL READ COMMITTED;

-- Decrement quantity by 5 for product_id 101
UPDATE Inventory SET quantity = quantity - 5 WHERE product_id = 101;

-- Commit Transaction 1
COMMIT;
```

Transaction 2 (Increment by 10):

```sql
-- Begin Transaction 2
START TRANSACTION;

-- Set Isolation Level for Transaction 2 (Read Committed)
SET TRANSACTION ISOLATION LEVEL READ COMMITTED;

-- Increment quantity by 10 for product_id 101
UPDATE Inventory SET quantity = quantity + 10 WHERE product_id = 101;

-- Commit Transaction 2
COMMIT;
```

Potential Inconsistencies without Isolation:

Without proper isolation levels, inconsistencies can occur due to concurrent access and updates:

Dirty Read: A transaction reads uncommitted changes made by another transaction.

Non-Repeatable Read: A transaction reads the same data twice but gets different results because of another transaction's changes.

Phantom Read: A transaction reads a set of rows twice, and the second read includes new rows inserted by another transaction.

To showcase the inconsistencies, run both transactions concurrently in separate sessions, and observe the results or use isolation levels such as **READ COMMITTED**, **REPEATABLE READ**, **SERIALIZABLE**, and examine the potential inconsistencies like incorrect quantities or changes visible before committed.

The specific results and observed inconsistencies may vary based on the isolation levels set, the timing of the transactions, and the database system's concurrency control mechanisms. Adjust the isolation levels and transaction contents based on your database system and requirements to observe different consistency issues.

Develop a view combining data from multiple tables, like merging employee details from one table with department information from another.

Solution:

Creating a view that combines data from multiple tables is a powerful way to consolidate information from different sources. Let's create a view that merges employee details from one table (**Employees**) with department information from another table (**Departments**).

Assuming the following table schemas:

Employees Table Schema:

```sql
CREATE TABLE Employees (
    employee_id INT PRIMARY KEY,
    employee_name VARCHAR(50),
    department_id INT,
    position VARCHAR(50),
    salary DECIMAL(10, 2)
);
```

Departments Table Schema:

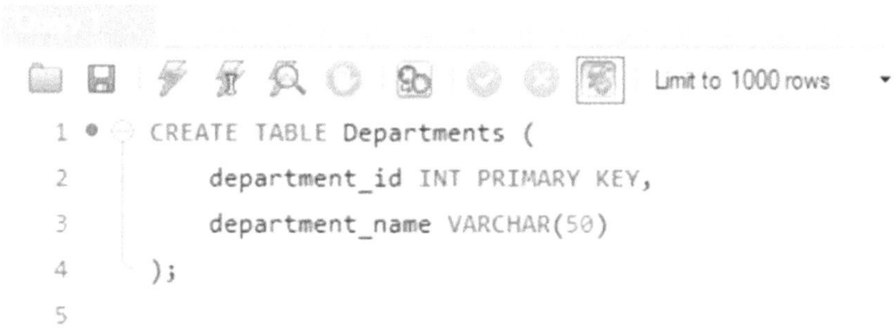

We'll create a view **EmployeeDepartmentView** that combines employee details with corresponding department names:

Creating the View:

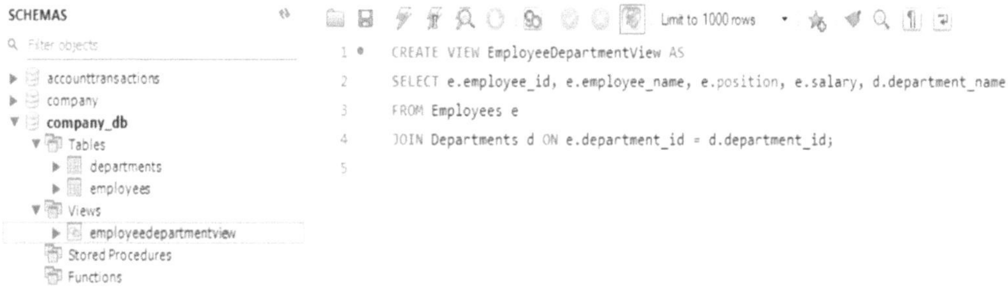

This view (**EmployeeDepartmentView**) fetches details such as **employee_id**, **employee_name**, **position**, **salary**, and **department_name** by joining the **Employees** and **Departments** tables on the **department_id** column.

You can query this view as you would query a regular table:

Querying the View:

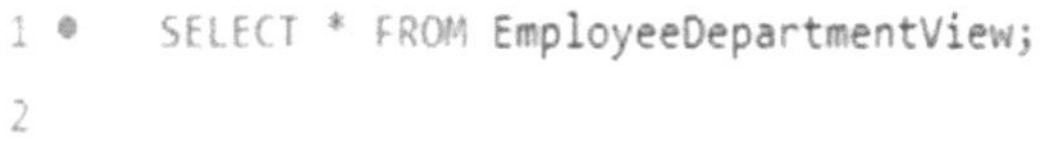

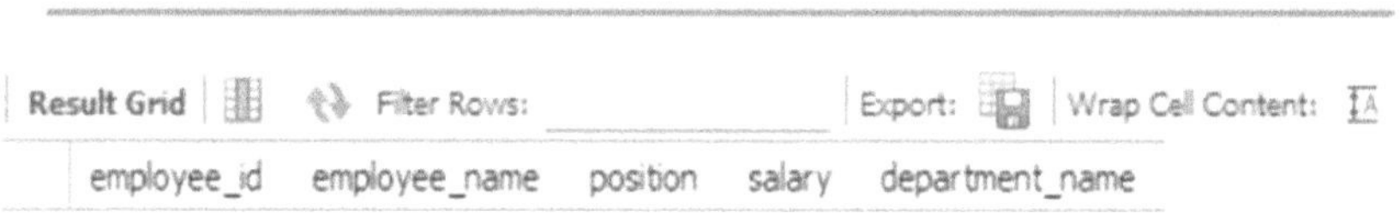

This will retrieve consolidated information, displaying employee details along with their respective department names.

Feel free to adjust the view columns, add more conditions or join multiple tables based on your specific data requirements.

Chapter 7 : Advanced Topics

Study and Implementation of
Replication in MySQL
High Availability and Failover
Security Best Practices
Backup and Recovery Strategies

Objective:
Understanding and implementing the process of replicating data across multiple MySQL servers to ensure data redundancy, scalability, and fault tolerance.
Implementing strategies to maintain database uptime, ensuring minimal downtime through failover mechanisms and redundancy configurations.
Implementing robust security measures to protect data integrity and confidentiality, including user access controls, encryption, and authentication mechanisms.
Establishing reliable backup methods and recovery procedures to safeguard against data loss and enable efficient restoration in case of failures.

LAB PRACTICE ASSIGNMENT:

Set up a MySQL cluster with multiple nodes to ensure high availability.

Solution:
Setting up a MySQL cluster involves configuring multiple nodes to ensure high availability and fault tolerance. MySQL Cluster typically uses the NDB (MySQL Cluster NDB) storage engine for achieving this. Here's a basic outline of how you can set up a MySQL Cluster:
Requirements:
Multiple servers/nodes (at least 3 for redundancy)
MySQL Cluster software installed on each node
Steps to Set Up MySQL Cluster:
Configure Node Types:
Identify nodes for management (management server), data storage (data nodes), and SQL access (SQL nodes).
Install MySQL Cluster software on each node and specify the type during installation.
Configuration File Setup:
Configure the **config.ini** or **my.cnf** files on each node:
Define node IDs, IP addresses, and port numbers.
Set up data node directories, management node addresses, etc.
Start Management Node:
Start the management server on a chosen node:
ndb_mgmd -f /path/to/config.ini --initial
Start Data Nodes:
Start data nodes on designated machines:
ndbd --initial
Start SQL Nodes:
Start SQL nodes to enable client connections:
mysqld --initial
Cluster Configuration and Monitoring:
Connect to the management node with **ndb_mgm** to monitor and manage the cluster.
Check cluster status:
ndb_mgm> show
Testing High Availability:
Simulate node failures and verify cluster resilience:
Shut down nodes and observe cluster failover and recovery.
Important Notes:

Ensure network settings allow communication between nodes.
Use proper firewall rules to secure cluster communication.
Properly handle backups, as traditional MySQL backup methods might differ for MySQL Cluster.
This outline provides a high-level overview of setting up a MySQL Cluster. Detailed configuration and specific commands might vary based on your environment and MySQL Cluster version. Refer to MySQL Cluster documentation or specific guides for a more comprehensive setup tailored to your needs.

Simulate a failover scenario by intentionally stopping a primary node and observing automatic failover to secondary nodes.

Solution:
To simulate a failover scenario in a MySQL Cluster, we'll intentionally stop a primary node and observe how the cluster handles the automatic failover to secondary nodes.
Scenario Setup:
Let's assume a basic setup with three nodes: one management node (**ndb_mgmd**) and two data nodes (**ndbd**). We'll simulate a failover scenario by stopping one of the data nodes and observe the cluster's behavior.
Steps to Simulate Failover:
Identify the Node to Stop:
Connect to the management node:
ndb_mgm
View the cluster status and identify the data node to stop:
SHOW
Stop a Data Node:
Select one of the data nodes (let's assume **ndbd** on node 2) and intentionally stop it:
ndb_mgm> 2 STOP
Monitor Cluster Status:
Observe the cluster status to witness the automatic failover and recovery process:
SHOW
Verify Failover and Recovery:
Check for changes in the cluster status and ensure the remaining node(s) take over the tasks of the stopped node.
Verify that the cluster remains operational, with the remaining nodes handling the workload without interruption.
Notes:
The cluster should automatically detect the failure of a data node and redistribute its data to ensure continued operation.
Automatic failover is a fundamental feature of MySQL Cluster, ensuring high availability by redistributing data and tasks among operational nodes in case of failures.
This simulation allows you to observe how the MySQL Cluster handles failover scenarios, ensuring that even if a primary node fails, the cluster remains operational by redistributing data and tasks to maintain high availability and resilience. Adjust the steps based on your specific cluster setup and requirements.

Create multiple user roles with different privileges.

Solution:
Creating multiple user roles with different privileges in MySQL involves using the **GRANT** statement to assign specific privileges to users. Here's an example of creating multiple roles:
Example:
Suppose you have different roles like **admin**, **analyst**, and **developer**.
Creating Roles:

```sql
-- Create users with appropriate roles
CREATE USER 'admin_user'@'%' IDENTIFIED BY 'password';
CREATE USER 'analyst_user'@'%' IDENTIFIED BY 'password';
CREATE USER 'developer_user'@'%' IDENTIFIED BY 'password';
```

Assigning Privileges:

Admin Role:

```sql
-- Grant all privileges to the admin role
GRANT ALL PRIVILEGES ON *.* TO 'admin_user'@'%';
```

Analyst Role:

```sql
-- Grant specific privileges to the analyst role
GRANT SELECT, INSERT, UPDATE ON database_name.* TO 'analyst_user'@'%';
```

Developer Role:

```sql
-- Grant privileges to the developer role
GRANT SELECT, INSERT, UPDATE, DELETE ON another_database.* TO 'developer_user'@'%';
```

Revoking Privileges (Optional):

If needed, you can revoke specific privileges from roles using the **REVOKE** statement.

Verifying Roles and Privileges:

```sql
-- Check user privileges
SHOW GRANTS FOR 'admin_user'@'%';
SHOW GRANTS FOR 'analyst_user'@'%';
SHOW GRANTS FOR 'developer_user'@'%';
```

Note:

Replace **'admin_user'**, **'analyst_user'**, **'developer_user'** with the actual usernames you want to create.
Modify the database names (**database_name**, **another_database**) and the list of privileges (**SELECT**, **INSERT**, **UPDATE**, **DELETE**) as per your requirements.
This way, different user roles (**admin**, **analyst**, **developer**) will have distinct sets of privileges within the MySQL database, allowing controlled access based on their respective roles and responsibilities. Adjust the privileges and databases according to your specific use case and security requirements.

Assign these roles to specific users and ensure they can only perform operations allowed by their roles.

Solution:
Assigning roles to specific users in MySQL involves associating each user with the appropriate role created earlier. Here's how you can assign roles and ensure they can only perform operations allowed by their respective roles:
Assigning Roles to Users:
Suppose we have users **admin_user**, **analyst_user**, and **developer_user**, and we want to assign them their respective roles:
Assigning Roles:
Admin User:
Assign the admin role to the admin user
GRANT admin_role TO 'admin_user'@'%';
Analyst User:
Assign the analyst role to the analyst user
GRANT analyst_role TO 'analyst_user'@'%';
Developer User:
Assign the developer role to the developer user
GRANT developer_role TO 'developer_user'@'%';
Verify Role Assignments:
Check role assignments for users
SELECT * FROM mysql.user WHERE User IN ('admin_user', 'analyst_user', 'developer_user');
Limiting Operations Based on Roles:
You've already defined privileges for each role earlier. MySQL will automatically limit users to operations allowed by their assigned roles:
Admin Role: Users assigned the **admin_role** will have full privileges (**ALL PRIVILEGES**).
Analyst Role: Users assigned the **analyst_role** will have limited privileges for specified operations (e.g., **SELECT**, **INSERT**, **UPDATE**).
Developer Role: Users assigned the **developer_role** will have their specified privileges (e.g., **SELECT**, **INSERT**, **UPDATE**, **DELETE**).
By assigning roles to users, MySQL will enforce the privileges granted to those roles, ensuring that users can only perform operations permitted by their respective roles. Adjust roles and user assignments based on your specific access control requirements.

Configure MySQL to use SSL for secure client-server communication.
Solution:
Configuring MySQL to use SSL (Secure Sockets Layer) for secure client-server communication involves several steps. Here's a high-level overview of the process:
Steps to Configure SSL for MySQL:
Enable SSL Support in MySQL Server:
Open your MySQL configuration file (**my.cnf** or **my.ini**).
Look for the **[mysqld]** section and add or modify the following lines:

```
[mysqld] ssl-ca=/path/to/ca-cert.pem ssl-cert=/path/to/server-cert.pem ssl-key=/path/to/server-key.pem
```

Generate SSL Certificates:
Generate SSL certificates for the MySQL server.
Create a Certificate Authority (CA) certificate: **ca-cert.pem**
Create a Server certificate signed by the CA: **server-cert.pem**
Create a private key for the server: **server-key.pem**
Secure Certificate Storage:

Ensure secure permissions for certificate files:

```
chmod 600 /path/to/server-key.pem chown mysql:mysql /path/to/*.pem
```

Restart MySQL Server:

Restart the MySQL server for changes to take effect:

```
systemctl restart mysql # For systemd-based systems
```

Client-Side Configuration:

Update client configurations (**my.cnf** or during client connection) to include SSL options:

```
[client] ssl-ca=/path/to/ca-cert.pem
```

Verify SSL Connection:

Connect to the MySQL server using SSL:

```
mysql -u username -p --ssl-ca=/path/to/ca-cert.pem --ssl-cert=/path/to/client-cert.pem --ssl-key=/path/to/client-key.pem
```

Notes:

Replace **/path/to/...** with the actual paths to your certificate files.

Ensure that MySQL's SSL-related options are set up correctly on both the server and client sides.

Adjust the SSL configuration based on your specific security requirements and network setup.

MySQL versions and configurations might slightly differ, so refer to the MySQL documentation for precise details based on your MySQL version.

Enabling SSL for MySQL ensures encrypted communication between MySQL clients and the server, enhancing security by protecting data exchanged during client-server interactions.

Verify that connections are encrypted using SSL by capturing and inspecting network traffic.

Solution:

Verifying SSL encryption in MySQL connections involves capturing and inspecting network traffic to confirm that data is encrypted. You can use tools like Wireshark to analyze the network packets. Here's an overview:

Steps to Verify SSL Encryption in MySQL Connections:

Prepare Wireshark:

Install Wireshark on your system if you haven't already.

Open Wireshark and select the network interface used by the MySQL server/client.

Capture Network Traffic:

Start capturing packets by clicking on the network interface.

Initiate a connection to the MySQL server using SSL from the client.

Filter Captured Traffic:

Apply a display filter to focus on MySQL-related traffic:

mysql || tls || ssl

This filter will display MySQL and SSL/TLS-related packets.

Inspect Packets:

Look for packets related to the MySQL connection.

Inspect the packets to confirm the presence of SSL/TLS handshake and encrypted data.

Verification Points:

Confirm that SSL handshake packets (like **Client Hello**and **Server Hello**) are present.

Check for packets containing encrypted MySQL query traffic.

Analysis:

Examine packet details to ensure SSL/TLS negotiation and encrypted data transfer between the client and server.

Verify that sensitive data exchanged between the client and server is encrypted.

Notes:

Wireshark will display SSL/TLS-related packet details, including handshake, cipher suites, and encrypted payload.

Look for packets using the MySQL default port (3306) and marked as SSL/TLS or MySQL protocol.

Confirm the absence of plain text data (queries, responses) in the captured packets.

By inspecting the network traffic using Wireshark or similar tools, you can visually verify SSL encryption in MySQL connections. This verification confirms that the communication between the MySQL client and server is encrypted and secure.

Set up a regular automated backup plan for databases.

Solution:

Setting up regular automated backups for MySQL databases can be achieved using various methods. One common approach is using cron jobs (on Linux) or Task Scheduler (on Windows) along with MySQL's **mysqldump** utility. Here's a basic guide:

Steps to Set Up Automated MySQL Database Backups:

Create Backup Script:

Create a shell script (Linux) or batch script (Windows) to execute the **mysqldump** command.

Include commands to dump specific databases or all databases, specifying backup paths and filenames.

For example, on Linux, create a **backup_script.sh**:

```
#!/bin/bash mysqldump -u your_username -pYour_Password your_database > /path/to/backup/backup.sql
```

Secure the Backup Script:

Ensure the script has appropriate permissions and store sensitive data (like passwords) securely.

Set Up Cron Job or Task Scheduler:

On Linux:

Edit crontab by running **crontab -e**.

Add a cron job to schedule backups:

```
0 3 * * * /path/to/backup_script.sh # Example: Daily backup at 3 AM
```

On Windows:

Use Task Scheduler to create a task that executes the batch script at scheduled intervals.

Testing:

Run the backup script manually to ensure it works as intended.

Check the backup file to confirm that it contains the database dump.

Retention Policy:

Consider implementing a retention policy to manage backup files and disk space.

Regularly purge old backups based on your retention strategy.

Log and Monitoring:

Implement logging mechanisms to track backup success/failure.

Monitor backups regularly to ensure they are running as scheduled.

Notes:

Modify the script to suit your specific database credentials, database names, backup paths, and backup schedules.

Use authentication methods other than embedding passwords directly into scripts for better security (e.g., MySQL configuration files, environment variables).

Regularly test and validate backups by restoring them to ensure data integrity.

Automating backups using scheduled tasks ensures that your MySQL databases are regularly backed up, reducing the risk of data loss in case of system failures or accidental data deletions. Adjust the backup frequency and strategies based on your data sensitivity and business requirements.

Test the backup process by restoring from the backup file to ensure data integrity.

Solution:

testing the backup integrity through a restore process is crucial. To validate the backup, follow these steps to restore a MySQL database from the backup file:

Steps to Test MySQL Backup Restoration:

Prepare the Backup File:

Ensure you have a recent backup file created using **mysqldump**.

Create a Test Database (Optional):

If you want to restore the backup to a test database:

```
CREATE DATABASE test_db;
```

Restore Database from Backup:

Using the backup file, restore the database:

```
mysql -u your_username -p test_db < /path/to/backup/backup.sql
```

Replace **your_username** with the MySQL username, **test_db** with the database name, and **/path/to/backup/backup.sql** with the actual path to your backup file.

Verification:

Access the restored database to confirm its existence:

```
mysql -u your_username -p test_db
```

Inspect Data:
Check tables and records within the restored database:
USE test_db;
SHOW TABLES; -- List tables
SELECT * FROM table_name; -- View records in tables
Data Integrity Check:
Compare the restored database's content with the original database to ensure data integrity.
Functional Testing (Optional):
Perform functional tests on the restored database to ensure that the application's functionality is intact.
Notes:
The restore process should be done in a test or staging environment to avoid any impact on production data.
Verify that the restored data matches the data from the original database to ensure data consistency and accuracy.
Regularly test backups by restoring them to different environments to ensure their reliability in case of actual data loss or system failure.
By regularly testing the restore process, you validate the integrity of your backups, ensuring they are usable in case of emergencies or data loss scenarios.

Perform a point-in-time recovery by restoring a database to a specific timestamp, utilizing the binary log files.

Solution:
Performing a point-in-time recovery (PITR) in MySQL involves restoring a database to a specific timestamp by utilizing the binary log files (also known as "binlogs"). Here's a basic overview of the process:
Steps for Point-in-Time Recovery using Binary Logs:
Enable Binary Logging:
Ensure that MySQL's binary logging is enabled in the server configuration (**my.cnf** or **my.ini**).

```
[mysqld] log_bin = /path/to/binlog_directory/binlog
```

Check Binary Logs:
List the available binary log files and note the timestamp you want to restore to:
SHOW BINARY LOGS;
Determine Target Timestamp:
Identify the timestamp or log sequence number (LSN) representing the point in time you want to restore the database to.
Restore Backup and Apply Binary Logs:
Restore the latest full backup of the database.
Apply binary logs to reach the desired point-in-time:

```
mysqlbinlog --start-datetime="YYYY-MM-DD HH:MM:SS" /path/to/binlog.001 | mysql -u your_username -p
your_database
```

Replace **YYYY-MM-DD HH:MM:SS** with the specific timestamp and **/path/to/binlog.001** with the correct binary log file containing data from or after the target time.
Verification:
Validate the database's state by checking records before and after the timestamp to ensure the restoration to the desired point-in-time.
Notes:
Ensure that you have a combination of full backups and binary log backups for PITR.
MySQL binary logs contain all changes made to the database after enabling binary logging, allowing you to perform point-in-time recoveries.
PITR is a complex process and requires a good understanding of your database and its transactional behaviour.
Consider practicing this in a non-production environment before performing it on critical systems.
Performing a point-in-time recovery using binary logs allows you to restore your MySQL database to a specific timestamp, enabling recovery to a precise point in time in case of data corruption or accidental data changes.

Simulate data loss and recover the lost data using MySQL's point-in-time recovery capabilities.

Solution:

Simulating data loss and performing a point-in-time recovery (PITR) in MySQL involves intentionally causing data loss and then recovering the lost data using binary logs. Here's a basic outline to simulate and recover lost data:

Simulating Data Loss:

Create a Test Database (if not already created):

```
CREATE DATABASE test_db; USE test_db;
```

Generate Test Data:

Create a table and insert some test data.

```
CREATE TABLE test_table (
id INT PRIMARY KEY AUTO_INCREMENT,
name VARCHAR(50)
);

INSERT INTO test_table (name) VALUES ('Record 1'), ('Record 2'), ('Record 3');
```

Delete or Modify Data:

Intentionally delete or modify records to simulate data loss.

```
DELETE FROM test_table WHERE id = 2; -- Simulate deletion of a specific record
```

OR

```
UPDATE test_table SET name = 'Modified Record' WHERE id = 3; -- Simulate modification
```

Performing Point-in-Time Recovery:

Check Binary Logs:

List available binary log files and their timestamps.

```
SHOW BINARY LOGS;
```

Identify Timestamp:

Identify the timestamp or log sequence number (LSN) before the data loss occurred.

Restore to a Specific Timestamp:

Restore the database to a point just before the data loss.

```
mysqlbinlog --stop-datetime="YYYY-MM-DD HH:MM:SS" /path/to/binlog.001 | mysql -u your_username -p your_database
```

Replace **YYYY-MM-DD HH:MM:SS** with the timestamp just before the data loss and **/path/to/binlog.001** with the appropriate binlog file.

Verification:

Check the **test_table** to confirm that the deleted or modified data has been recovered.

Notes:

Simulating data loss should be performed in a controlled environment, preferably in a test or staging database.

PITR requires an understanding of binary logs, timestamps, and the sequence of events.

Practice caution while using production data for testing and make sure you have proper backups before intentionally causing data loss.

This process allows you to intentionally cause data loss in a MySQL database and then use the point-in-time recovery capabilities to restore the lost data by applying binary logs up to a specific timestamp before the data loss occurred.

Chapter 8 : MySQL and Application Integration

Study and Implementation of
Using MySQL with Programming Languages (e.g., PHP, Python)
Connecting MySQL with Web Applications
Integrating MySQL with Other Systems (e.g., APIs)

Objective:
Integrate MySQL with programming languages (PHP, Python, etc.) to perform CRUD (Create, Read, Update, Delete) operations.
Utilize MySQL APIs/libraries in PHP/Python for database operations.
Understand MySQL integration within web applications for data storage and retrieval.
Integrate MySQL databases with external systems or APIs for data exchange.

LAB PRACTICE ASSIGNMENT:

Create a PHP script to establish a connection with a MySQL database.

Solution:
PHP script that establishes a connection with a MySQL database using MySQLi (MySQL Improved) extension:

```
<?php
$servername = "localhost"; // Replace with your MySQL server's hostname or IP address
$username = "your_username"; // Replace with your MySQL username
$password = "your_password"; // Replace with your MySQL password
$dbname = "your_database"; // Replace with your database name

// Create connection
$conn = new mysqli($servername, $username, $password, $dbname);

// Check connection
if ($conn->connect_error) {
die("Connection failed: " . $conn->connect_error);
} else {
echo "Connected successfully";
}

// Close the connection (optional)
$conn->close();
?>
```

Replace the placeholders (**your_username**, **your_password**, **your_database**, **localhost**) with your actual MySQL credentials and database details.
Explanation:
$servername, **$username**, **$password**, and **$dbname** hold the connection details.
mysqli is used to establish the connection with the MySQL server using these credentials.
The **connect_error** property checks if there's an error in connecting to the database.
If the connection fails, it displays an error message. Otherwise, it confirms the successful connection.
This script can be expanded to execute SQL queries, perform CRUD operations, or handle other database-related tasks once the connection is established successfully. Always ensure to handle sensitive information securely, especially in production environments.

Perform a simple SELECT query in PHP to retrieve and display data from a MySQL table.

Solution:
Executing a simple SELECT query in PHP to retrieve and display data from a MySQL table:

```php
<?php
$servername = "localhost";  // Replace with your MySQL server's hostname or IP address
$username = "your_username"; // Replace with your MySQL username
$password = "your_password"; // Replace with your MySQL password
$dbname = "your_database"; // Replace with your database name

// Create connection
$conn = new mysqli($servername, $username, $password, $dbname);

// Check connection
if ($conn->connect_error) {
die("Connection failed: " . $conn->connect_error);
}

// SQL query
$sql = "SELECT * FROM your_table"; // Replace 'your_table' with the actual table name

// Execute query and fetch results
$result = $conn->query($sql);

if ($result->num_rows > 0) {
// Output data of each row
while($row = $result->fetch_assoc()) {
echo "ID: " . $row["id"] . " - Name: " . $row["name"] . "<br>"; // Adjust column names accordingly
}
} else {
echo "0 results";
}

// Close the connection
$conn->close();
?>
```

Replace the placeholders (**your_username**, **your_password**, **your_database**, **localhost**, **your_table**) with your actual MySQL credentials, database details, and table name.

Explanation:

Establishes a connection to the MySQL database.

Constructs a SELECT query to retrieve all columns from a specified table.

Executes the query using **$conn->query($sql)** and checks if there are any rows returned.

If rows are found, it loops through the results and displays them.

Finally, it closes the database connection.

Ensure that you have the appropriate table and column names in the query and adjust the output (**echo**) to match your table's structure. This script retrieves and displays data from the specified table in the database.

Write a Python script to connect to a MySQL database using pymysql.

Solution:

First, make sure you have **pymysql** installed. If not, you can install it via pip:

```
pip install pymysql
```

Next, here's a Python script that establishes a connection with a MySQL database using pymysql:

```python
import pymysql

# Database connection details
hostname = 'localhost'  # Replace with your MySQL server's hostname or IP address
username = 'your_username'  # Replace with your MySQL username
password = 'your_password'  # Replace with your MySQL password
database = 'your_database'  # Replace with your database name
```

```
try:
# Establish connection to MySQL
conn = pymysql.connect(
host=hostname,
user=username,
password=password,
database=database
)

# Create a cursor object to interact with the database
cursor = conn.cursor()

# Check if the connection is successful
if conn.open:
print("Connected to MySQL!")

# Close the cursor and connection
cursor.close()
conn.close()

except pymysql.MySQLError as e:
print(f"Error connecting to MySQL: {e}")
```

Replace the placeholders (**your_username**, **your_password**, **your_database**, **localhost**) with your actual MySQL credentials and database details.

Explanation:

Import the **pymysql** module.

Define database connection details.

Establish a connection to the MySQL database using **pymysql.connect()**.

Create a cursor object to execute SQL queries.

Print a success message if the connection is established.

Close the cursor and connection.

Catch any MySQL-related errors that might occur during the connection attempt.

This script demonstrates how to establish a connection to a MySQL database using **pymysql** in Python. Adjust the error handling and further database operations based on your requirements.

Implement CRUD operations in Python (e.g., insert data, fetch data, update records).

Solution:

Implementing CRUD (Create, Read, Update, Delete) operations using **pymysql** in Python:

Ensure you have a table named **employees** with columns **id**, **name**, **designation**, and **joining_date** in your database.

```
import pymysql

# Database connection details
hostname = 'localhost'  # Replace with your MySQL server's hostname or IP address
username = 'your_username'  # Replace with your MySQL username
password = 'your_password'  # Replace with your MySQL password
database = 'your_database'  # Replace with your database name

# Function to establish a connection
def connect_to_db():
return pymysql.connect(host=hostname, user=username, password=password, database=database)

# Create operation: Insert data into the database
def insert_employee(name, designation, joining_date):
try:
conn = connect_to_db()
```

```
cursor = conn.cursor()
sql = "INSERT INTO employees (name, designation, joining_date) VALUES (%s, %s, %s)"
cursor.execute(sql, (name, designation, joining_date))
conn.commit()
print("Record inserted successfully!")
except pymysql.Error as e:
print(f"Error inserting record: {e}")
finally:
cursor.close()
conn.close()

# Read operation: Fetch data from the database
def fetch_employees():
try:
conn = connect_to_db()
cursor = conn.cursor()
sql = "SELECT * FROM employees"
cursor.execute(sql)
rows = cursor.fetchall()
for row in rows:
print(f"ID: {row[0]}, Name: {row[1]}, Designation: {row[2]}, Joining Date: {row[3]}")
except pymysql.Error as e:
print(f"Error fetching data: {e}")
finally:
cursor.close()
conn.close()

# Update operation: Modify existing record in the database
def update_employee(employee_id, new_designation):
try:
conn = connect_to_db()
cursor = conn.cursor()
sql = "UPDATE employees SET designation = %s WHERE id = %s"
cursor.execute(sql, (new_designation, employee_id))
conn.commit()
print("Record updated successfully!")
except pymysql.Error as e:
print(f"Error updating record: {e}")
finally:
cursor.close()
conn.close()

# Call functions to perform operations
insert_employee("John Doe", "Manager", "2023-11-16")
fetch_employees()
update_employee(1, "Senior Manager")
fetch_employees()
```

Replace the placeholders (**your_username**, **your_password**, **your_database**, **localhost**) with your actual MySQL credentials and database details.

This script demonstrates how to:

Insert a record into the **employees** table.

Fetch all records from the **employees** table.

Update a specific record in the **employees** table.

You can extend this script by adding delete functionality or refining the operations based on your requirements.

Create a simple web application using PHP that connects to a MySQL database.

Solution:
PHP web application that connects to a MySQL database and fetches data to display on a web page.
Assuming you have a table named **employees** with columns **id**, **name**, **designation**, and **joining_date** in your MySQL database.

```
<!DOCTYPE html>
<html>
<head>
<title>Employee Records</title>
</head>
<body>

<h2>Employee Records</h2>

<?php
$servername = "localhost"; // Replace with your MySQL server's hostname or IP address
$username = "your_username"; // Replace with your MySQL username
$password = "your_password"; // Replace with your MySQL password
$dbname = "your_database"; // Replace with your database name

// Create connection
$conn = new mysqli($servername, $username, $password, $dbname);

// Check connection
if ($conn->connect_error) {
die("Connection failed: " . $conn->connect_error);
}

// Fetch employee records
$sql = "SELECT * FROM employees";
$result = $conn->query($sql);

if ($result->num_rows > 0) {
echo "<table border='1'>";
echo "<tr><th>ID</th><th>Name</th><th>Designation</th><th>Joining Date</th></tr>";
while ($row = $result->fetch_assoc()) {
echo "<tr>";
echo "<td>" . $row["id"] . "</td>";
echo "<td>" . $row["name"] . "</td>";
echo "<td>" . $row["designation"] . "</td>";
echo "<td>" . $row["joining_date"] . "</td>";
echo "</tr>";
}
echo "</table>";
} else {
echo "0 results";
}

// Close connection
$conn->close();
?>

</body>
</html>
```

Replace the placeholders (**your_username**, **your_password**, **your_database**, **localhost**) with your actual MySQL credentials and database details.

Explanation:
This PHP script establishes a connection to the MySQL database and fetches employee records from the **employees** table.
It creates an HTML table to display the fetched records on a web page.
If the connection is successful and there are records, it displays them in the table format; otherwise, it shows "0 results".
Save this script with a **.php** extension and run it on a PHP-enabled server to see the employee records displayed on the webpage. Adjust the layout and styling as needed.

Implement a form to insert user-submitted data into the MySQL database upon submission.

Solution:
Assuming you have a table named **employees** with columns **name**, **designation**, and **joining_date** in your MySQL database.

```
<!DOCTYPE html>
<html>
<head>
<title>Insert Employee Record</title>
</head>
<body>

<h2>Insert Employee Record</h2>

<form action="insert.php" method="post">
<label for="name">Name:</label>
<input type="text" id="name" name="name" required><br><br>

<label for="designation">Designation:</label>
<input type="text" id="designation" name="designation" required><br><br>

<label for="joining_date">Joining Date:</label>
<input type="date" id="joining_date" name="joining_date" required><br><br>

<input type="submit" value="Submit">
</form>

</body>
</html>
```

This HTML form includes fields for **name**, **designation**, and **joining_date**, and a submit button. The form **action** attribute is set to **insert.php**, which is the PHP file where we'll handle the insertion of data into the database.
Now, create a PHP file named **insert.php** to handle the form submission and insert data into the database:

```
<?php
$servername = "localhost"; // Replace with your MySQL server's hostname or IP address
$username = "your_username"; // Replace with your MySQL username
$password = "your_password"; // Replace with your MySQL password
$dbname = "your_database"; // Replace with your database name

// Create connection
$conn = new mysqli($servername, $username, $password, $dbname);

// Check connection
if ($conn->connect_error) {
die("Connection failed: " . $conn->connect_error);
}

// Get form data
```

```
$name = $_POST['name'];
$designation = $_POST['designation'];
$joining_date = $_POST['joining_date'];

// Insert data into the database
$sql = "INSERT INTO employees (name, designation, joining_date) VALUES ('$name', '$designation', '$joining_date')";

if ($conn->query($sql) === TRUE) {
echo "New record inserted successfully";
} else {
echo "Error: " . $sql . "<br>" . $conn->error;
}

// Close connection
$conn->close();
?>
```

Replace the placeholders (**your_username**, **your_password**, **your_database**, **localhost**) with your actual MySQL credentials and database details.

This PHP script handles the form submission, retrieves the form data using **$_POST**, and inserts it into the **employees** table in the database. Upon submission, it will display a success message or an error message if the insertion fails.

Ensure both files (**insert.html** and **insert.php**) are in the same directory. Access **insert.html** in a browser, fill in the form, and submit it to insert data into the MySQL database. Adjust the code as needed for error handling, validation, and security.

Develop an HTML page with JavaScript (AJAX) to fetch and display data from a MySQL database asynchronously.

Solution:

Assuming you have a table named **employees** with columns **name**, **designation**, and **joining_date** in your MySQL database.

HTML File (**index.html**):

```
<!DOCTYPE html>
<html>
<head>
<title>Display Employee Records</title>
<script>
function fetchData() {
var xhr = new XMLHttpRequest();

xhr.onreadystatechange = function() {
if (xhr.readyState === 4 && xhr.status === 200) {
document.getElementById("result").innerHTML = xhr.responseText;
}
};

xhr.open("GET", "fetch.php", true);
xhr.send();
}
</script>
</head>
<body>

<h2>Display Employee Records</h2>
```

```
<button onclick="fetchData()">Fetch Data</button>

<div id="result"></div>

</body>
</html>
```

JavaScript:

The HTML file contains a button to trigger the data fetching process.

When the button is clicked, the **fetchData()** function is executed.

This function uses AJAX (XMLHttpRequest) to make an asynchronous GET request to the server (to **fetch.php**).

PHP File (**fetch.php**):

```
<?php
$servername = "localhost"; // Replace with your MySQL server's hostname or IP address
$username = "your_username"; // Replace with your MySQL username
$password = "your_password"; // Replace with your MySQL password
$dbname = "your_database"; // Replace with your database name

// Create connection
$conn = new mysqli($servername, $username, $password, $dbname);

// Check connection
if ($conn->connect_error) {
die("Connection failed: " . $conn->connect_error);
}

// Fetch employee records
$sql = "SELECT * FROM employees";
$result = $conn->query($sql);

if ($result->num_rows > 0) {
echo "<table border='1'>";
echo "<tr><th>Name</th><th>Designation</th><th>Joining Date</th></tr>";
while ($row = $result->fetch_assoc()) {
echo "<tr>";
echo "<td>" . $row["name"] . "</td>";
echo "<td>" . $row["designation"] . "</td>";
echo "<td>" . $row["joining_date"] . "</td>";
echo "</tr>";
}
echo "</table>";
} else {
echo "0 results";
}

// Close connection
$conn->close();
?>
```

Replace the placeholders (**your_username**, **your_password**, **your_database**, **localhost**) with your actual MySQL credentials and database details.

This setup will asynchronously fetch data from the **employees** table in your MySQL database and display it in a table format on the web page when the "Fetch Data" button is clicked. Adjust the code as needed for error handling and security measures. Both HTML and PHP files should be in the same directory.

Develop a simple RESTful API using a framework like Flask (Python) or Express (Node.js) to perform CRUD operations on a MySQL database.

Solution:

Ensure you have Flask installed. You can install it via pip:

pip install Flask

Here's an example:

```
from flask import Flask, request, jsonify
import mysql.connector

app = Flask(__name__)

# Database configuration
db = mysql.connector.connect(
host="localhost",
user="your_username",
passwd="your_password",
database="your_database"
)

cursor = db.cursor()

# Create employee table if not exists
cursor.execute("CREATE TABLE IF NOT EXISTS employees (id INT AUTO_INCREMENT PRIMARY KEY,
name VARCHAR(255), designation VARCHAR(255), joining_date DATE)")

# API endpoints

# Get all employees
@app.route('/employees', methods=['GET'])
def get_employees():
cursor.execute("SELECT * FROM employees")
employees = cursor.fetchall()
if len(employees) > 0:
return jsonify(employees)
else:
return jsonify({'message': 'No employees found'})

# Get employee by ID
@app.route('/employees/<int:id>', methods=['GET'])
def get_employee(id):
cursor.execute("SELECT * FROM employees WHERE id = %s", (id,))
employee = cursor.fetchone()
if employee:
return jsonify(employee)
else:
return jsonify({'message': 'Employee not found'})

# Add new employee
@app.route('/employees', methods=['POST'])
def add_employee():
data = request.get_json()
name = data['name']
designation = data['designation']
joining_date = data['joining_date']

cursor.execute("INSERT INTO employees (name, designation, joining_date) VALUES (%s, %s, %s)", (name,
designation, joining_date))
db.commit()
```

```
return jsonify({'message': 'Employee added successfully'})

# Update employee by ID
@app.route('/employees/<int:id>', methods=['PUT'])
def update_employee(id):
data = request.get_json()
name = data['name']
designation = data['designation']
joining_date = data['joining_date']

cursor.execute("UPDATE employees SET name = %s, designation = %s, joining_date = %s WHERE id = %s", (name, designation, joining_date, id))
db.commit()

return jsonify({'message': 'Employee updated successfully'})

# Delete employee by ID
@app.route('/employees/<int:id>', methods=['DELETE'])
def delete_employee(id):
cursor.execute("DELETE FROM employees WHERE id = %s", (id,))
db.commit()

return jsonify({'message': 'Employee deleted successfully'})

if __name__ == '__main__':
app.run(debug=True)
```

Replace **your_username**, **your_password**, and **your_database** with your MySQL credentials.
This example creates a simple API with routes for CRUD operations on an **employees** table in a MySQL database. You can test the endpoints using tools like Postman or by sending HTTP requests.
Ensure MySQL is running and accessible. This example is a basic setup; in production, consider adding security measures, error handling, and validation checks for input data.

Explore using Google Sheets API or similar services to fetch data from a MySQL database and populate a Google Sheet.

Solution:
To integrate Google Sheets with a MySQL database, you can use Google Sheets API along with Python to fetch data from the database and populate a Google Sheet. Here's a basic example using the **gspread** library, which facilitates Google Sheets integration in Python.
Firstly, ensure you have the necessary libraries installed:
Install the **gspread** library:

```
pip install gspread
```

Enable the Google Sheets API and create credentials for your project on the Google Developers Console to obtain a JSON file with authentication details.
Here's a sample Python script to fetch data from a MySQL database and populate a Google Sheet:

```
import gspread
from oauth2client.service_account import ServiceAccountCredentials
import mysql.connector

# MySQL configuration
db = mysql.connector.connect(
host="localhost",
user="your_username",
passwd="your_password",
database="your_database"
```

```
)

cursor = db.cursor()

# Google Sheets configuration
scope = ['https://spreadsheets.google.com/feeds', 'https://www.googleapis.com/auth/drive']
creds = ServiceAccountCredentials.from_json_keyfile_name('your_credentials.json', scope)  # Replace with your JSON credentials file
client = gspread.authorize(creds)

# Open the Google Sheets spreadsheet
spreadsheet = client.open('Your Spreadsheet Name')  # Replace with your Google Sheets document name

# Select the first sheet
sheet = spreadsheet.sheet1

# Fetch data from MySQL database
cursor.execute("SELECT * FROM your_table")  # Replace with your table name
data = cursor.fetchall()

# Insert data into Google Sheets starting from cell A1
for i, row in enumerate(data):
for j, value in enumerate(row):
sheet.update_cell(i + 1, j + 1, value)

print("Data imported to Google Sheets successfully!")
```

Replace **your_username**, **your_password**, **your_database**, **your_credentials.json**, and **Your Spreadsheet Name** with your MySQL credentials, database name, Google credentials file, and the name of the Google Sheets document, respectively.

This script fetches data from the MySQL database and populates a Google Sheet starting from cell A1 with the fetched data. Adjust it according to your table structure and the range where you want to insert data in Google Sheets.

Ensure the JSON credentials file is in the same directory as your script or provide the correct path to the file.

Be mindful of sensitive data and authentication details when handling credentials and avoid sharing them publicly.

Implement user authentication systems in PHP/Python applications connected to MySQL databases.

Solution:

Implementing user authentication involves several steps and considerations. Here's an overview of how you might set up a basic user authentication system using PHP and a MySQL database.

Steps to Implement User Authentication:

Database Setup:

Create a **users** table in your MySQL database to store user credentials (username, password hash, etc.).

Hash and store passwords securely using hashing algorithms like bcrypt.

Registration Page:

Create a registration form (HTML/PHP) where users can sign up by providing necessary details like username and password.

Upon form submission, hash the password and store the user data in the **users** table.

Login Page:

Create a login form (HTML/PHP) where users can enter their credentials (username and password).

Validate the entered credentials against the stored data in the **users** table.

If the credentials match, authenticate the user and create a session to maintain their logged-in state.

Session Management:

Upon successful login, create a session for the user to persist their login state across pages.

Set session variables to store user information (e.g., user ID, username) to validate access to restricted areas.

Access Control:

Implement access control mechanisms to restrict certain pages or functionalities to authenticated users. Check the user's session to determine if they have the necessary permissions to access specific resources.

Logout Functionality:

Create a logout mechanism that destroys the session and logs the user out.

Example (PHP):

Registration (register.php):

```
<?php
// Process registration form submission
if ($_SERVER["REQUEST_METHOD"] == "POST") {
// Validate form data

// Hash the password securely
$hashedPassword = password_hash($_POST["password"], PASSWORD_BCRYPT);

// Store user data in the 'users' table
// Implement your MySQL database connection here
// Example query: INSERT INTO users (username, password) VALUES ($_POST["username"], $hashedPassword);

// Redirect to login page or any other page
}
?>
```

Login (login.php):

```
<?php
// Process login form submission
session_start();
if ($_SERVER["REQUEST_METHOD"] == "POST") {
// Validate form data and check credentials against the 'users' table
// Retrieve user data using the provided username

if (/* Check if password matches */) {
// Authentication successful
$_SESSION["username"] = $username; // Store user information in session
header("Location: dashboard.php"); // Redirect to the dashboard or a protected area
} else {
// Invalid credentials, display an error message
}
}
?>
```

This is a high-level overview, and real implementations would involve more considerations like password strength, CSRF protection, and secure session handling. Always use prepared statements to prevent SQL injection.

For a secure and production-ready implementation, consider using established frameworks like Laravel (PHP) or Django (Python), which provide built-in authentication features and robust security measures.

Chapter 9: Case Studies and Projects

Study and Implementation of
Case Studies on Real-World MySQL Implementations
Project Assignments for Hands-on Practice

Objective:
Case studies and project assignments enable learners to apply theoretical knowledge to real-world scenarios, fostering a deeper understanding of MySQL implementation practices and enhancing practical skills in database design, optimization, and application development.

LAB PRACTICE ASSIGNMENT:

Investigate how an e-commerce platform (e.g., Amazon, eBay) structures its MySQL databases for product catalog, user management, transactions, and order processing.

Solution:
Investigating how large e-commerce platforms structure their MySQL databases involves understanding their database schema, which can be intricate due to the scale and complexity of operations. While specific details aren't publicly disclosed, here's a generalized overview of how such platforms might structure their databases:
Product Catalog:
Products Table: Contains details of each product (e.g., product ID, name, description, price, stock quantity, categories, attributes).
Categories Table: Stores hierarchical categories for organizing products.
Images Table: Holds references to product images or thumbnails.
Attributes Table: If products have various attributes (size, color), this table stores such information.
User Management:
Users Table: Stores user information (username, email, hashed passwords, shipping addresses, payment details).
Roles and Permissions: A table that manages user roles and permissions for admin, customers, sellers, etc.
Transactions and Orders:
Orders Table: Contains details of each order (order ID, user ID, date, status).
Order Items Table: Stores items within each order (order item ID, order ID, product ID, quantity, price).
Payments Table: Information about payments made (payment ID, order ID, amount, payment status, payment method).
Cart and Checkout:
Shopping Cart Table: Stores temporary cart items before checkout.
Checkout Table: Handles checkout process, contains shipping details, and finalizes orders.
Reviews and Ratings:
Reviews Table: Stores user reviews and ratings for products.
Ratings Table: May contain aggregate data or ratings on products.
Analytics and Logs:
Logs Table: Records system logs, user activities, and interactions.
Analytics Table: Stores data for analytics purposes, like user behavior, sales trends, etc.
Miscellaneous:
Sessions Table: Handles user sessions for website functionality.
Caching Tables: Temporary tables for caching frequently accessed data to improve performance.
For such platforms, scalability, data integrity, and performance are critical. They likely use indexing, partitioning, caching mechanisms, and might employ advanced techniques like sharding or replication for handling large datasets and ensuring high availability.
Understanding the specific schema and optimizations used by large e-commerce platforms would require direct access or detailed documentation, which is usually proprietary and not publicly available.

Analyze techniques used for optimizing queries, handling high traffic, and ensuring data consistency and reliability.

Solution:
Optimizing queries, managing high traffic, and ensuring data consistency and reliability are critical aspects of database management, especially in scenarios like e-commerce platforms or large-scale applications. Below are techniques commonly used to address these challenges:
Query Optimization:
Indexing: Efficient indexing of frequently queried columns improves query performance.
Query Execution Plan: Analyzing and optimizing the query execution plan to reduce query response time.
Normalization and Denormalization: Balancing between normalized databases for data integrity and denormalization for performance gains.
Stored Procedures: Using stored procedures or prepared statements to reduce network traffic and improve performance.
Query Caching: Caching query results to minimize repetitive query execution.
High Traffic Handling:
Scaling Techniques: Employing horizontal (adding more servers) or vertical (upgrading server resources) scaling to handle increased traffic.
Load Balancing: Distributing traffic across multiple servers to improve performance and reliability.
Caching Strategies: Implementing caching layers (Redis, Memcached) to store frequently accessed data and reduce database load.
Content Delivery Networks (CDNs): Utilizing CDNs for caching and delivering static assets closer to users.
Data Consistency and Reliability:
Transactions and ACID Properties: Ensuring Atomicity, Consistency, Isolation, and Durability in database operations to maintain data integrity.
Replication: Employing database replication for redundancy and high availability.
Backup and Recovery Strategies: Implementing regular backups and recovery plans to safeguard against data loss.
Monitoring and Alerts: Setting up monitoring tools and alerts to detect and address issues proactively.
Consistent Hashing: Employing consistent hashing techniques to distribute load evenly across servers while minimizing data movement during node addition/removal.
Data Partitioning and Sharding:
Horizontal Partitioning: Dividing large tables into smaller ones (based on range, list, or hash) to improve manageability and query performance.
Sharding: Distributing data across multiple databases or servers (based on a shard key) to reduce load on individual servers and improve scalability.
Redundancy and Failover Mechanisms:
Database Clustering: Implementing database clustering to ensure high availability and failover support.
Automated Failover: Configuring systems to automatically switch to backup servers in case of primary server failure.
Implementing these techniques requires a deep understanding of the application's architecture, database structure, and specific requirements to effectively optimize performance, handle traffic spikes, and maintain data consistency and reliability.

Explore the database schema and design principles employed by healthcare information systems (e.g., patient records, medical history, appointments) utilizing MySQL.

Solution:
Healthcare information systems involve intricate database schemas to manage patient data, medical records, appointments, and more. Here's a generalized view of how MySQL might structure such systems:
Patient Information:
Patients Table: Contains patient details (patient ID, name, contact, address, insurance information).
Medical Records Table: Stores medical history, diagnoses, allergies, surgeries, medications, lab results, etc.
Insurance Table: Information related to insurance providers, policy numbers, coverage details.
Appointments and Scheduling:
Appointments Table: Contains details about scheduled appointments (appointment ID, patient ID, doctor ID, date/time, reason).
Doctors Table: Stores information about doctors, their specialties, contact details, schedules, etc.
Departments Table: Information on different departments or specialties within the healthcare facility.

Treatment and Procedures:
Procedures Table: Lists medical procedures, codes, descriptions, costs.
Prescriptions Table: Tracks prescribed medications, dosage, frequency, and associated patient information.
Imaging and Reports:
Imaging Records Table: Stores imaging reports, scans, X-rays, and related metadata.
Lab Tests Table: Information on lab tests, results, dates, and patient details.
Administrative Data:
Staff Table: Information about hospital staff, their roles, contact details, etc.
Facility Information: Contains details about hospitals, clinics, or healthcare facilities.
Relationships and Linkages:
Foreign Keys: Establishes relationships between tables (e.g., patient ID in Medical Records links to Patients Table).
Views: Utilized for complex queries and simplified access to joined data from multiple tables.
Security and Compliance:
Access Control: Enforces security measures to restrict access to sensitive patient data based on roles.
Audit Trails: Records changes and accesses to patient data for compliance purposes.
Encryption: Protects sensitive data (e.g., health records) to meet security and privacy standards.
Compliance and Standards:
HIPAA Compliance: Ensures compliance with regulations for protecting patient health information.
Data Integrity Checks: Implements checks to maintain data accuracy and consistency.
Miscellaneous:
Reports Table: Stores generated reports, summaries, or analytics derived from patient data.
System Logs: Tracks system activities, errors, and maintenance logs for auditing purposes.
The design principles focus on data integrity, accessibility, security, and adherence to healthcare regulations like HIPAA to ensure patient confidentiality and privacy. The schema may evolve to accommodate specific healthcare provider needs and regulations while ensuring efficient data management and retrieval.

Focus on security measures, compliance with regulations (e.g., HIPAA), and efficient data retrieval strategies.

Solution:
Healthcare information systems, security measures and compliance with regulations like HIPAA (Health Insurance Portability and Accountability Act) are paramount. Here's a more detailed perspective on security, compliance, and efficient data retrieval strategies:
Security Measures:
Access Control: Implement role-based access control (RBAC) to restrict data access based on user roles (e.g., doctors, nurses, administrators).
Encryption: Use encryption methods (such as AES encryption) for sensitive data at rest and during transmission to prevent unauthorized access.
Authentication and Authorization: Employ strong authentication mechanisms (like multi-factor authentication) and granular authorization to ensure only authorized personnel access patient data.
Secure Development Practices: Follow secure coding practices to prevent common vulnerabilities like SQL injection, cross-site scripting (XSS), etc.
Regular Security Audits: Conduct regular security audits and vulnerability assessments to identify and address potential threats or weaknesses.
Compliance with HIPAA Regulations:
Patient Privacy: Ensure strict adherence to patient privacy guidelines, safeguarding Protected Health Information (PHI) from unauthorized access or disclosure.
Data Encryption: Encrypt sensitive patient data both at rest and during transmission.
Audit Trails: Maintain audit logs to track access to patient data, modifications, and system activities for compliance and accountability.
Risk Assessments: Conduct periodic risk assessments to identify vulnerabilities and mitigate potential risks to patient data security.
Efficient Data Retrieval Strategies:
Indexing: Create appropriate indexes on frequently queried columns to speed up data retrieval.
Normalization and Denormalization: Balance between normalized database structure for data integrity and denormalization for improved query performance.

Optimized Queries: Write efficient SQL queries, utilize EXPLAIN to analyze query execution plans, and optimize accordingly.
Caching Mechanisms: Implement caching (e.g., using Redis) to store frequently accessed data and reduce database load.
Data Partitioning: Use horizontal partitioning or sharding to distribute data across servers for faster retrieval.
Data Retention and Backup:
Data Retention Policies: Implement policies for retaining and purging patient data based on regulatory requirements and operational needs.
Backup and Recovery: Set up regular backups and robust recovery mechanisms to prevent data loss and ensure continuity in case of system failures.
These measures collectively help in maintaining data integrity, ensuring patient confidentiality, meeting regulatory requirements, and optimizing data retrieval, crucial in healthcare systems where access to accurate patient information is critical for patient care and treatment.

Examine how social media platforms (e.g., Facebook, Twitter) manage massive user data, interactions, and content storage using MySQL.

Solution:
Social media platforms like Facebook and Twitter handle vast amounts of user-generated data, interactions, and content storage. MySQL plays a significant role in managing these massive databases. Here's an overview of how they might structure their databases:
User Data Management:
Users Table: Contains user profile information (user ID, name, username, email, hashed passwords, etc.).
Connections/Friends Table: Stores relationships between users (follower-followee relationships for Twitter, friends for Facebook).
Interactions and Activities:
Posts Table: Stores user-generated content, including posts, tweets, status updates, etc. (post ID, content, timestamp, likes, shares, comments).
Likes/Reactions Table: Records user engagements, such as likes, reactions, or upvotes on posts.
Comments Table: Stores comments on posts or tweets, linking back to the post ID and user ID.
Shares/Retweets Table: Records instances where users share or retweet content, indicating the source content and the user who shared it.
Content Storage:
Media Table: Stores multimedia content (images, videos, etc.) uploaded by users, linked to respective posts or tweets.
External Links Table: Records links shared within posts or tweets.
Analytics and Recommendations:
Activity Logs: Tracks user activities, engagement metrics, and interactions for analytics and recommendations.
Recommendation System Data: Stores information used for personalized content recommendations based on user behavior.
Messaging Systems (In case of Facebook):
Messenger Tables: Stores conversation history, messages, and metadata related to user-to-user or group chats.
Optimization and Scalability:
Sharding: Horizontal partitioning of data across multiple servers to handle scalability.
Caching Mechanisms: Use of caching layers (like Memcached or Redis) to enhance performance and reduce database load.
Replication: Replicating databases across multiple servers for fault tolerance and performance.
Security and Compliance:
Access Controls: Implement strict access controls to protect user data, allowing only authorized personnel to access specific data.
Data Encryption: Encrypt sensitive data to ensure user privacy and compliance with regulations.
These platforms use MySQL in conjunction with other technologies and optimizations to efficiently handle the enormous volume of data, ensuring rapid access, real-time interactions, and reliable storage of user-generated content while maintaining high availability and scalability to accommodate millions or even billions of users.

Study methods for horizontal scaling, handling multimedia content, and maintaining data integrity in a high-throughput environment.

Solution:

In a high-throughput environment with multimedia content, maintaining data integrity and scaling horizontally are crucial challenges. Here are some methods and considerations:

Horizontal Scaling:

Sharding: Partition data horizontally across multiple servers based on a shard key (e.g., user ID, geographical location) to distribute the load evenly.

Database Partitioning: Divide tables vertically or horizontally to distribute data across multiple servers based on specific criteria (e.g., columns, ranges).

Load Balancing: Use load balancers to distribute incoming traffic among multiple database servers to avoid overload and evenly distribute query loads.

Replication: Set up database replication to create copies of the database across multiple servers for improved read performance and fault tolerance.

Microservices Architecture: Implement microservices where each service manages a specific function or set of functionalities, allowing for independent scaling of services.

Handling Multimedia Content:

Separate Storage: Store multimedia content (images, videos) in separate storage systems (like object storage or CDN) and store references/pointers in the database.

Use of Content Delivery Networks (CDNs): Cache and deliver multimedia content from edge servers closer to users, reducing server load and improving content delivery speed.

File Metadata Storage: Store metadata related to multimedia content in the database (e.g., file name, type, size, location).

Compression and Optimization: Compress multimedia files before storage to reduce storage space and optimize content delivery.

Maintaining Data Integrity:

ACID Compliance: Ensure Atomicity, Consistency, Isolation, and Durability properties for database transactions to maintain data integrity.

Data Validation: Implement strict data validation rules and constraints to ensure data accuracy and prevent invalid data entry.

Backup and Recovery: Regularly back up data and implement robust recovery mechanisms to prevent data loss and maintain integrity in case of failures.

Concurrency Control: Use mechanisms like locking or optimistic concurrency control to manage simultaneous access to data and prevent conflicts or inconsistencies.

High-Throughput Considerations:

Optimized Queries: Write efficient queries, utilize indexing, and optimize database design to handle high-throughput demands efficiently.

Caching Mechanisms: Implement caching layers to store frequently accessed data and reduce the load on the database servers.

Asynchronous Processing: Employ asynchronous processing for non-critical tasks (e.g., background jobs, data processing) to prevent bottlenecks in the main processing flow.

By employing these strategies, organizations can effectively scale their databases horizontally, handle multimedia content efficiently, and maintain data integrity in high-throughput environments, ensuring robust performance and reliability.

Project Assignments for Hands-on Practice:

Online Bookstore Management System:

Design and implement a MySQL database for an online bookstore, including tables for books, authors, customers, orders, and inventory.

Create SQL scripts for CRUD operations, search functionalities, and generating reports.

Inventory Management System for a Retail Store:

Develop a MySQL database schema for managing product inventory, suppliers, sales, and orders for a retail store.

Implement stored procedures or triggers for automating inventory updates or reordering processes.

Blog or Content Management Platform:

Build a MySQL database schema for a blogging platform or content management system (CMS).

Include tables for articles, authors, categories, comments, and user roles with appropriate relationships.

Implementation Guidelines:

Encourage documentation detailing the database schema, ER diagrams, query optimizations, and performance tuning strategies.

Emphasize normalization, indexing, and efficient data retrieval methods in the project assignments.

Allow students to work in groups or individually, providing a real-world problem to solve with MySQL.

Chapter 10 : Appendix

Study and Implementation of
MySQL Command Line Interface (CLI) Reference
Troubleshooting Common MySQL Issues
Glossary of Terms

Objective:
Familiarize with essential MySQL CLI commands for database management.
Understand and resolve frequent MySQL problems.
Compile a comprehensive glossary defining MySQL-related terminology.

LAB PRACTICE ASSIGNMENT:

Create a reference guide outlining basic CLI commands (e.g., mysql, use, show, create, select, insert, update, delete).
Solution:
Here's a basic reference guide outlining essential MySQL Command Line Interface (CLI) commands:
Connecting to MySQL:
mysql -u [username] -p: Initiates MySQL and prompts for the user's password.
Database Operations:
SHOW DATABASES;: Displays all available databases.
USE [database_name];: Chooses a specific database for use.
CREATE DATABASE [database_name];: Generates a new database.
DROP DATABASE [database_name];: Removes an existing database.
Table Operations:
SHOW TABLES;: Lists all tables in the selected database.
DESCRIBE [table_name]; or **DESC [table_name];:** Shows the structure of a table.
CREATE TABLE [table_name] ([column_name] [data_type], ...);: Creates a new table.
DROP TABLE [table_name];: Deletes an existing table.
Data Manipulation:
SELECT [column_name(s)] FROM [table_name];: Retrieves data from a table.
INSERT INTO [table_name] ([column_name(s)]) VALUES (value1, value2, ...);: Inserts new records into a table.
UPDATE [table_name] SET [column_name] = [new_value] WHERE [condition];: Modifies existing records in a table.
DELETE FROM [table_name] WHERE [condition];: Deletes records from a table.
Other Commands:
QUIT or **EXIT;:** Closes the MySQL command line interface.
HELP;: Displays MySQL help information.
STATUS;: Shows the current status of the MySQL server.
USE;: Indicates the currently selected database.
SOURCE [file_path];: Executes SQL statements from a file.
These commands are instrumental for interacting with MySQL via the command line interface. Note that these commands are case-insensitive but conventionally written in uppercase for clarity. Adjustments to commands might be necessary based on specific SQL versions or configurations.

Include explanations and examples demonstrating the usage of each command for database creation, table manipulation, data retrieval, and user management.

Solution:
Connecting to MySQL:
mysql -u [username] -p: Initiates MySQL and prompts for the user's password.
Database Operations:
SHOW DATABASES;: Displays all available databases.

Example: **SHOW DATABASES;**
USE [database_name];: Chooses a specific database for use.
Example: **USE my_database;**
CREATE DATABASE [database_name];: Generates a new database.
Example: **CREATE DATABASE my_database;**
DROP DATABASE [database_name];: Removes an existing database.
Example: **DROP DATABASE my_database;**
Table Operations:
SHOW TABLES;: Lists all tables in the selected database.
Example: **SHOW TABLES;**
DESCRIBE [table_name]; or **DESC [table_name];:** Shows the structure of a table.
Example: **DESC my_table;**
CREATE TABLE [table_name] ([column_name] [data_type], ...);: Creates a new table.
Example:
```
CREATE TABLE employees (
id INT AUTO_INCREMENT PRIMARY KEY,
name VARCHAR(50),
age INT,
department VARCHAR(50)
);
```
DROP TABLE [table_name];: Deletes an existing table.
Example: **DROP TABLE employees;**
Data Manipulation:
SELECT [column_name(s)] FROM [table_name];: Retrieves data from a table.
Example: **SELECT * FROM employees;**
INSERT INTO [table_name] ([column_name(s)]) VALUES (value1, value2, ...);: Inserts new records into a table.
Example:
```
INSERT INTO employees (name, age, department)
VALUES ('John', 30, 'Sales');
```
UPDATE [table_name] SET [column_name] = [new_value] WHERE [condition];: Modifies existing records in a table.
Example:
```
UPDATE employees
SET department = 'Marketing'
WHERE name = 'John';
```
DELETE FROM [table_name] WHERE [condition];: Deletes records from a table.
Example:
```
DELETE FROM employees
WHERE name = 'John';
```
User Management:
CREATE USER [username] IDENTIFIED BY '[password]';: Creates a new user.
Example: **CREATE USER 'new_user' IDENTIFIED BY 'password123';**
GRANT [privileges] ON [database_name].[table_name] TO [username];: Grants specific privileges to a user.
Example: **GRANT SELECT, INSERT ON my_database.employees TO 'new_user';**
REVOKE [privileges] ON [database_name].[table_name] FROM [username];: Revokes privileges from a user.
Example: **REVOKE SELECT ON my_database.employees FROM 'new_user';**
These commands enable you to interact with MySQL through the command line, facilitating database creation, table manipulation, data retrieval, and user management. Adjust syntax and parameters as per your specific database structure and requirements.

Compile a troubleshooting guide addressing common issues (e.g., connection errors, performance bottlenecks, access privileges).
Solution:
Connection Errors:
Error: Can't connect to MySQL server on 'localhost' (10061):

Solution: Check if the MySQL server is running. Verify the correct port (default: 3306) and ensure it's not blocked by a firewall.
Error: Access denied for user 'username'@'localhost' (using password: YES):
Solution: Verify the username, password, and host. Ensure the user has the necessary privileges to access the database.
Performance Bottlenecks:
Slow Query Performance:
Solution: Use **EXPLAIN** before queries to analyze execution plans. Index frequently queried columns. Optimize complex queries, avoiding unnecessary joins or subqueries.
High CPU/Memory Usage:
Solution: Identify resource-intensive queries using monitoring tools. Optimize queries or consider hardware upgrades for better performance.
Access Privileges:
Error: Access denied; you need (at least one of) the [privileges] privilege(s) for this operation:
Solution: Ensure the user has the necessary privileges. Grant required privileges using **GRANT**.
Disk Space Issues:
Error: The table is full:
Solution: Check available disk space. Optimize table sizes, consider archiving or deleting old data, or extend disk storage.
Data Integrity and Corruption:
Error: Table 'table_name' is marked as crashed and should be repaired:
Solution: Use **REPAIR TABLE** command to fix corrupted tables. Regularly perform backups to mitigate data loss.
General Tips:
Check Logs: Review MySQL error logs (**error.log**) for detailed error messages.
Restart Services: Try restarting the MySQL service to resolve minor issues.
Upgrade MySQL: Consider upgrading to the latest stable version for bug fixes and enhancements.
Backup Regularly: Maintain regular backups to prevent data loss in case of failures.
Seeking Further Help:
Official Documentation: Consult MySQL official documentation for detailed solutions and troubleshooting steps.
Online Communities: Seek help from MySQL forums or communities where experts provide guidance for specific issues.
MySQL Support: Consider professional support services offered by MySQL for complex issues.
Remember to back up your data before performing any troubleshooting steps that might affect the database. Always test solutions in a non-production environment first.

Include step-by-step solutions and diagnostic commands to resolve each issue, covering topics like slow queries, disk space errors, or authentication problems.

Solution:
Connection Errors:
Issue: Can't connect to MySQL server on 'localhost'
Solution Steps:
Check MySQL Service Status:
Command: **sudo systemctl status mysql**
If stopped, start MySQL service: **sudo systemctl start mysql**
Verify MySQL Port and Firewall:
Command: **sudo netstat -tuln | grep 3306**
Ensure port 3306 (default MySQL port) is open and MySQL is listening.
Issue: Access denied for user 'username'@'localhost'
Solution Steps:
Check User Credentials:
Ensure the username, password, and host are correct.
Command: **mysql -u username -p**
Grant User Privileges:
Access MySQL as a privileged user: **mysql -u root -p**
Grant privileges: **GRANT ALL ON *.* TO 'username'@'localhost';**

Performance Bottlenecks:
Issue: Slow Query Performance
Solution Steps:
Explain Query Execution Plan:
Command: **EXPLAIN SELECT ...**
Analyze the query's execution plan to identify bottlenecks.
Index Optimization:
Analyze existing indexes: **SHOW INDEX FROM table_name;**
Add missing indexes for frequently queried columns: **CREATE INDEX index_name ON table_name(column_name);**
Issue: High CPU/Memory Usage
Solution Steps:
Monitor MySQL Processlist:
Command: **SHOW PROCESSLIST;**
Identify long-running queries or processes consuming resources.
Optimize Queries:
Analyze and optimize high-resource-consuming queries.
Consider query caching or upgrading hardware resources if necessary.
Access Privileges:
Issue: Access denied; you need (at least one of) the [privileges] privilege(s)
Solution Steps:
Check User Privileges:
Command: **SHOW GRANTS FOR 'username'@'localhost';**
Grant necessary privileges: **GRANT SELECT ON database.* TO 'username'@'localhost';**
Disk Space Issues:
Issue: Table is full or Out of Disk Space
Solution Steps:
Check Disk Space:
Command: **df -h**
Identify available disk space and partitions.
Optimize Tables:
Identify large tables: **SELECT table_name, table_rows FROM information_schema.tables WHERE table_schema = 'your_database';**
Optimize or archive old data to free up space.
Data Integrity and Corruption:
Issue: Table is marked as crashed and should be repaired
Solution Steps:
Check Table Status:
Command: **CHECK TABLE table_name;**
Identify crashed tables: **REPAIR TABLE table_name;**
Diagnostic Tools and Logs:
MySQL Error Log Location:/var/log/mysql/error.log
Slow Query Log: Enable in **my.cnf** and review for performance issues.
Seeking Further Help:
Official MySQL Documentation: Detailed solutions and references to resolve specific issues.
Online Communities: MySQL forums or communities where experts provide guidance.
MySQL Support: Consider professional support services offered by MySQL.
Always perform a backup before executing critical commands and consider testing solutions in a non-production environment to avoid potential data loss or service disruption.

Create a glossary containing key MySQL terms, including definitions, explanations, and usage contexts.
Solution:
MySQL Glossary:
Database:
Definition: A structured collection of data organized for efficient retrieval.
Usage:CREATE DATABASE database_name;

Table:
Definition: A structured set of data elements organized in rows and columns.
Usage:CREATE TABLE table_name (column1 datatype, column2 datatype);
Column:
Definition: A vertical entity within a table that contains all information associated with a specific field.
Usage:ALTER TABLE table_name ADD column_name datatype;
Row:
Definition: A horizontal entity within a table that represents a record.
Usage:INSERT INTO table_name (column1, column2) VALUES (value1, value2);
Primary Key:
Definition: A unique identifier for a row in a table.
Usage:CREATE TABLE table_name (id INT PRIMARY KEY, ...);
Foreign Key:
Definition: A column in a table that references the primary key in another table.
Usage:FOREIGN KEY (column_name) REFERENCES another_table(pk_column);
Index:
Definition: A data structure that improves the speed of data retrieval operations on a table.
Usage:CREATE INDEX index_name ON table_name(column_name);
Query:
Definition: A request for data or information from a database.
Usage:SELECT * FROM table_name WHERE condition;
SQL (Structured Query Language):
Definition: A standard language used to communicate with and manage databases.
Usage:SELECT, INSERT, UPDATE, DELETE
DDL (Data Definition Language):
Definition: SQL commands that define, alter, or drop database objects.
Usage:CREATE, ALTER, DROP
DML (Data Manipulation Language):
Definition: SQL commands that manipulate data within database objects.
Usage:SELECT, INSERT, UPDATE, DELETE
ACID Properties:
Definition: Atomicity, Consistency, Isolation, Durability - the characteristics ensuring database transaction reliability.
Usage: Ensuring transactions are reliably processed.
Transaction:
Definition: A logical unit of work that contains one or more SQL statements.
Usage:BEGIN TRANSACTION; ... COMMIT;
View:
Definition: A virtual table derived from other tables.
Usage:CREATE VIEW view_name AS SELECT...
Stored Procedure:
Definition: A set of SQL statements stored in the database and executed together.
Usage:CREATE PROCEDURE procedure_name AS...
Trigger:
Definition: A set of actions that are automatically performed when specified events occur.
Usage:CREATE TRIGGER trigger_name...
Replication:
Definition: The process of copying data from one database to another to maintain redundancy.
Usage: Setting up Master-Slave replication.
High Availability:
Definition: Ensuring a system is always operational and accessible with minimal downtime.
Usage: Implementing failover systems.

Feel free to expand or customize this glossary according to your needs, including additional terms or more detailed explanations where necessary!

Cover terms related to database structure (e.g., schema, table, column), SQL concepts (e.g., JOIN, index, normalization), and administrative aspects (e.g., user privileges, replication).

Solution:
Database Structure:
Schema:
Definition: A logical container for database objects, including tables, views, indexes, etc.
Usage:CREATE SCHEMA schema_name;
Table:
Definition: A structured collection of data organized into rows and columns.
Usage:CREATE TABLE table_name (column1 datatype, column2 datatype);
Column:
Definition: A data element within a table that represents a specific attribute.
Usage:ALTER TABLE table_name ADD column_name datatype;
Row:
Definition: A horizontal entity within a table that represents a single record.
Usage:INSERT INTO table_name (column1, column2) VALUES (value1, value2);
Index:
Definition: A data structure that enhances the speed of data retrieval operations on a table.
Usage:CREATE INDEX index_name ON table_name(column_name);
Normalization:
Definition: Organizing data in a database to minimize redundancy and dependency.
Usage: Breaking down large tables into smaller ones to reduce duplication.
Denormalization:
Definition: Adding redundant data to improve query performance.
Usage: Storing derived data alongside base data for faster retrieval.
SQL Concepts:
JOIN:
Definition: A clause used to combine rows from two or more tables based on a related column.
Usage:SELECT * FROM table1 INNER JOIN table2 ON table1.column = table2.column;
Primary Key:
Definition: A unique identifier for a row in a table.
Usage:CREATE TABLE table_name (id INT PRIMARY KEY, ...);
Foreign Key:
Definition: A column that references a primary key in another table.
Usage:FOREIGN KEY (column_name) REFERENCES another_table(pk_column);
Transaction:
Definition: A logical unit of work that contains one or more SQL statements.
Usage:BEGIN TRANSACTION; ... COMMIT;
Subquery:
Definition: A query nested within another query.
Usage:SELECT * FROM table WHERE column IN (SELECT column FROM another_table);
Administrative Aspects:
User Privileges:
Definition: Permissions granted to users to perform specific actions on a database.
Usage:GRANT SELECT, INSERT ON database.table TO 'user'@'localhost';
Replication:
Definition: The process of copying data from one database to another.
Usage: Setting up Master-Slave replication for redundancy.
Backup and Recovery:
Definition: Strategies for creating data backups and restoring data in case of loss.
Usage: Regularly scheduled backups using **mysqldump** and restoring data from backups.

Chapter 11: Previous Years Questions and Answers

Create the following tables with the fields given below: (IGNOU BCA 2018)
TEACHER (T_ID, Department, Year of Exp, Name)
SUBJECT PAPER (Sub_Paper_ID, T_ID, Title_of Paper, Programme, Semester)
Select appropriate primary keys. Input at least 5 meaningful records in the tables. Select appropriate data types for all the fields.

Answer:

TEACHER table

```
CREATE TABLE TEACHER (
T_ID INT PRIMARY KEY,
Department VARCHAR(50),
Year_of_Exp INT,
Name VARCHAR(100)
);
```

SUBJECT PAPER table

```
CREATE TABLE SUBJECT_PAPER (
Sub_Paper_ID INT PRIMARY KEY,
T_ID INT,
Title_of_Paper VARCHAR(100),
Programme VARCHAR(50),
Semester VARCHAR(20),
FOREIGN KEY (T_ID) REFERENCES TEACHER(T_ID)
);
```

Insert records into TEACHER table

```
INSERT INTO TEACHER VALUES
(1010, 'Computer Science', 8, 'John Doe'),
(1020, 'Physics', 6, 'Jane Smith'),
(1030, 'Mathematics', 4, 'Alice Johnson'),
(1040, 'Computer Science', 10, 'Bob Williams'),
(1050, 'Physics', 7, 'Charlie Brown');
```

Insert records into SUBJECT_PAPER table

```
INSERT INTO SUBJECT_PAPER VALUES
(1, 1010, 'Database Management', 'BCA', '3rd Semester'),
(2, 1010, 'Programming in Java', 'BCA', '4th Semester'),
(3, 1020, 'Mechanics', 'BCA', '2nd Semester'),
(4, 1040, 'C Programming', 'BCA', '2nd Semester'),
(5, 1050, 'Electromagnetism', 'BCA', '3rd Semester');
```

For the tables designed in Question above, answer the following queries using SQL: (IGNOU BCA 2018)
Display Name and Year-Of-Exp of all the teachers of "Computer Science" department.

```
SELECT Name, Year_of_Exp
FROM TEACHER
WHERE Department = 'Computer Science';
```

Display name of teacher and department of all the teachers who have more than 5 years of experience.

```
SELECT Name, Department
FROM TEACHER
WHERE Year_of_Exp > 5;
```

List the file of Subject Paper which are handled by T_ID = 1010.

```
SELECT Title_of_Paper
FROM SUBJECT_PAPER
WHERE T_ID = 1010;
```

List the name of Programme and Semester of paper titled "C Programming".

```
SELECT Programme, Semester
FROM SUBJECT_PAPER
WHERE Title_of_Paper = 'C Programming';
```

List name of all the teachers of "Physics" department.

```
SELECT Name
FROM TEACHER
WHERE Department = 'Physics';
```

Create the following tables with the fields given below: (IGNOU BCA 2017)
STU_DETAILS (ENO, SNAME, DOB, ADDR1, ADDR2, CITY, COUNTRY)
MARK_DETAILS (ENO, MARKS1, MARKS2, MARKS3, TOTAL)
Select an appropriate primary key. Input at least 10 meaningful records. Select appropriate data types for all the fields.
Answer:
To create the tables **STU_DETAILS** and **MARK_DETAILS** as specified, along with selecting appropriate primary keys and data types, and inputting meaningful records, you can follow the SQL statements outlined below.
Table Creation:

STU_DETAILS Table:

```
CREATE TABLE STU_DETAILS (
ENO INT PRIMARY KEY,
SNAME VARCHAR(100),
DOB DATE,
ADDR1 VARCHAR(150),
ADDR2 VARCHAR(150),
CITY VARCHAR(50),
COUNTRY VARCHAR(50)
);
```

In this table, **ENO** (Enrollment Number) is a suitable primary key as it uniquely identifies each student. The data type for **DOB** (Date of Birth) is **DATE**, and for other text fields, **VARCHAR** with varying lengths is used.

MARK_DETAILS Table:

```
CREATE TABLE MARK_DETAILS (
ENO INT PRIMARY KEY,
MARKS1 INT,
MARKS2 INT,
MARKS3 INT,
TOTAL INT,
FOREIGN KEY (ENO) REFERENCES STU_DETAILS(ENO)
);
```

Here, **ENO** is also used as a primary key and it's a foreign key referencing **ENO** in **STU_DETAILS**. The marks and total are integers.

Inserting Records:

Inserting into **STU_DETAILS**:

```
INSERT INTO STU_DETAILS VALUES
(1001, 'John Doe', '2001-01-15', '123 Oak Street', 'Apt 4', 'New York', 'USA'),
(1002, 'Jane Smith', '2000-06-24', '456 Maple Avenue', '', 'Los Angeles', 'USA'),
(1003, 'Alice Johnson', '1999-03-10', '789 Pine Road', 'Suite 5', 'Chicago', 'USA'),
...; -- Continue for more records
```

Inserting into **MARK_DETAILS**:

```
INSERT INTO MARK_DETAILS VALUES
(1001, 85, 90, 87, 262),
(1002, 78, 81, 77, 236),
(1003, 92, 88, 91, 271),
...; -- Continue for more records
```

Remember to maintain consistency between the **ENO** in **STU_DETAILS** and **MARK_DETAILS** for referential integrity. Also, make sure the data inserted makes sense (e.g., total marks should be the sum of the individual marks). You can continue this pattern to input at least 10 meaningful records in each table.

For the above tables designed in Q.3, answer the following queries using SQL: (IGNOU BCA 2017)
To display the student's name of the student who scored the highest TOTAL.

```
SELECT S.SNAME
FROM STU_DETAILS S
JOIN MARK_DETAILS M ON S.ENO = M.ENO
ORDER BY M.TOTAL DESC
LIMIT 1;
```

To display the MARKS1 of all the students.

```
SELECT ENO, MARKS1
FROM MARK_DETAILS;
```

To display the ENOs of all the students who scored >50 marks in MARKS2.

```
SELECT ENO
FROM MARK_DETAILS
WHERE MARKS2 > 50;
```

Alter the table MARK_DETAILS to add a column AVG with appropriate data type.

```
ALTER TABLE MARK_DETAILS
ADD AVG FLOAT;
```

Using appropriate command drop the column COUNTRY from STU_DETAILS.

```
ALTER TABLE STU_DETAILS
DROP COLUMN COUNTRY;
```

Create the following tables with the fields given below : (IGNOU BCA 2017)
TEACHER (ID, Name, Dep_ID, Subject, Experience_in_years)
DEPARTMENT(Dep_ID, D_Name, Address, City)

Select appropriate primary keys. Input at least 5 meaningful records in the tables. Select appropriate data types for all the fields.
Answer:
Table Creation:
TEACHER Table:

```
CREATE TABLE TEACHER (
ID INT PRIMARY KEY,
Name VARCHAR(100),
Dep_ID INT,
Subject VARCHAR(100),
Experience_in_years INT
);
```

DEPARTMENT Table:

```
CREATE TABLE DEPARTMENT (
Dep_ID INT PRIMARY KEY,
D_Name VARCHAR(100),
Address VARCHAR(150),
City VARCHAR(50)
);
```

Inserting Records:

Inserting into **DEPARTMENT**:

```
INSERT INTO DEPARTMENT VALUES
(1, 'Computer Science', '123 Tech Road', 'Techville'),
(2, 'Mathematics', '456 Math Lane', 'Calcville'),
(3, 'Physics', '789 Quantum Blvd', 'Physicsburg'),
(4, 'Chemistry', '101 Chemical St', 'Chemtown'),
(5, 'Biology', '202 Bio Ave', 'BioCity');
```

Inserting into **TEACHER**:

```
INSERT INTO TEACHER VALUES
(101, 'John Doe', 1, 'Computer Networks', 5),
(102, 'Jane Smith', 2, 'Algebra', 3),
(103, 'Alice Johnson', 3, 'Thermodynamics', 7),
(104, 'Bob Williams', 4, 'Organic Chemistry', 4),
(105, 'Charlie Brown', 5, 'Molecular Biology', 6);
```

For the tables designed in question no. 5 above, answer the following queries using SQL: (IGNOU BCA 2017)
List the names of all the teachers who teach "Computer Science" and have more than 10 years of experience.

```
SELECT T.Name
FROM TEACHER T
JOIN DEPARTMENT D ON T.Dep_ID = D.Dep_ID
WHERE D.D_Name = 'Computer Science' AND T.Experience_in_years > 10;
```

List the addresses of all the "Physics Department" in city "Delhi".

```
SELECT Address
FROM DEPARTMENT
```

```
WHERE D_Name = 'Physics' AND City = 'Delhi';
```

Add column Date_of Birth in the TEACHER table.

```
ALTER TABLE TEACHER
ADD Date_of_Birth DATE;
```

Display the names and addresses of all the teachers of "Computer Science" who work for "Dep_ID = 110011".

```
SELECT T.Name, D.Address
FROM TEACHER T
JOIN DEPARTMENT D ON T.Dep_ID = D.Dep_ID
WHERE D.D_Name = 'Computer Science' AND T.Dep_ID = 110011;
```

Display the names and subjects of all the teachers whose experience is less than 5 years.

```
SELECT Name, Subject
FROM TEACHER
WHERE Experience_in_years < 5;
```

Create the following database defined below: (IGNOU BCA 2016)
SUPPLIER (Supplier #, Company_Name, City)
PARTS (Part #, Weight)
SUPPLY_PARTS (Supplier #, Part #)
PROJECTS (Project #, Part #, Quantity)
ORDERS (Part #, Supplier #, Date_of_Delivery)
Select appropriate datatypes for each of the fields. Input meaningful data of at least 10 records.
Answer:
Table Creation:
SUPPLIER Table:

```
CREATE TABLE SUPPLIER (
Supplier_Num INT PRIMARY KEY,
Company_Name VARCHAR(100),
City VARCHAR(50)
);
```

PARTS Table:

```
CREATE TABLE PARTS (
Part_Num INT PRIMARY KEY,
Weight DECIMAL(5,2)
);
```

SUPPLY_PARTS Table:

```
CREATE TABLE SUPPLY_PARTS (
Supplier_Num INT,
Part_Num INT,
PRIMARY KEY (Supplier_Num, Part_Num),
FOREIGN KEY (Supplier_Num) REFERENCES SUPPLIER(Supplier_Num),
FOREIGN KEY (Part_Num) REFERENCES PARTS(Part_Num)
);
```

PROJECTS Table:

```
CREATE TABLE PROJECTS (
Project_Num INT,
Part_Num INT,
Quantity INT,
PRIMARY KEY (Project_Num, Part_Num),
FOREIGN KEY (Part_Num) REFERENCES PARTS(Part_Num)
);
```

ORDERS Table:

```
CREATE TABLE ORDERS (
Part_Num INT,
Supplier_Num INT,
Date_of_Delivery DATE,
PRIMARY KEY (Part_Num, Supplier_Num),
FOREIGN KEY (Part_Num) REFERENCES PARTS(Part_Num),
FOREIGN KEY (Supplier_Num) REFERENCES SUPPLIER(Supplier_Num)
);
```

Inserting Records:
Inserting into **SUPPLIER**:

```
INSERT INTO SUPPLIER VALUES
(1, 'Company A', 'New York'),
(2, 'Company B', 'Los Angeles'),
...; -- Continue for more records
```

Inserting into **PARTS**:

```
INSERT INTO PARTS VALUES
(101, 5.75),
(102, 3.50),
...; -- Continue for more records
```

Inserting into **SUPPLY_PARTS**:

```
INSERT INTO SUPPLY_PARTS VALUES
(1, 101),
(2, 102),
...; -- Continue for more records
```

Inserting into **PROJECTS**:

```
INSERT INTO PROJECTS VALUES
(1001, 101, 20),
(1002, 102, 15),
...; -- Continue for more records
```

Inserting into **ORDERS**:

```
INSERT INTO ORDERS VALUES
(101, 1, '2024-01-15'),
(102, 2, '2024-02-20'),
...; -- Continue for more records
```

For the above database created in Q7, answer the following queries using SQL: (IGNOU BCA 2016)
Find all the parts supplied by supplier "123".

```
SELECT P.Part_Num
FROM SUPPLY_PARTS SP
JOIN PARTS P ON SP.Part_Num = P.Part_Num
WHERE SP.Supplier_Num = 123;
```

Find the cities where supplier "324" is located.

```
SELECT City
FROM SUPPLIER
WHERE Supplier_Num = 324;
```

Find another supplier who supplies at least one part supplied by supplier "431".

```
SELECT DISTINCT SP1.Supplier_Num
FROM SUPPLY_PARTS SP1
JOIN SUPPLY_PARTS SP2 ON SP1.Part_Num = SP2.Part_Num AND SP1.Supplier_Num != SP2.Supplier_Num
WHERE SP2.Supplier_Num = 431;
```

Find all the projects where part "P7" is used.

```
SELECT Project_Num
FROM PROJECTS
WHERE Part_Num = 'P7';
```

Find all the suppliers who supplies part "P5".

```
SELECT S.Supplier_Num, S.Company_Name
FROM SUPPLY_PARTS SP
JOIN SUPPLIER S ON SP.Supplier_Num = S.Supplier_Num
WHERE SP.Part_Num = 'P5';
```

Create the following database defined below : (IGNOU BCA 2016)
EMPLOYEE (ENo, EName, Birth_Date, Address, DNo)
DEPARTMENT (DNo, DName, DManager)
DEPT_LOCATION (DNo, DLocation, Country)
WORKS_ON (ENo, PNo, Hours)
PROJECT (PName, PNo, PLocation, DNo)
Select appropriate datatypes for each of the fields. Input meaningful data of at least 10 records.
Answer:
Table Creation:
EMPLOYEE Table:

```
CREATE TABLE EMPLOYEE (
ENo INT PRIMARY KEY,
EName VARCHAR(100),
Birth_Date DATE,
Address VARCHAR(150),
DNo INT
);
```

DEPARTMENT Table:

```
CREATE TABLE DEPARTMENT (
```

```
DNo INT PRIMARY KEY,
DName VARCHAR(100),
DManager INT
);
```

DEPT_LOCATION Table:

```
CREATE TABLE DEPT_LOCATION (
DNo INT,
DLocation VARCHAR(100),
Country VARCHAR(50),
PRIMARY KEY (DNo, DLocation),
FOREIGN KEY (DNo) REFERENCES DEPARTMENT(DNo)
);
```

WORKS_ON Table:

```
CREATE TABLE WORKS_ON (
ENo INT,
PNo INT,
Hours DECIMAL(5,2),
PRIMARY KEY (ENo, PNo),
FOREIGN KEY (ENo) REFERENCES EMPLOYEE(ENo),
FOREIGN KEY (PNo) REFERENCES PROJECT(PNo)
);
```

PROJECT Table:

```
CREATE TABLE PROJECT (
PName VARCHAR(100),
PNo INT PRIMARY KEY,
PLocation VARCHAR(100),
DNo INT,
FOREIGN KEY (DNo) REFERENCES DEPARTMENT(DNo)
);
```

Inserting Records:
Inserting into **DEPARTMENT**:

```
INSERT INTO DEPARTMENT VALUES
(1, 'IT', 101),
(2, 'HR', 102),
...; -- Continue for more records
```

Inserting into **EMPLOYEE**:

```
INSERT INTO EMPLOYEE VALUES
(1001, 'John Doe', '1985-01-15', '123 Oak Street', 1),
(1002, 'Jane Smith', '1990-06-24', '456 Maple Avenue', 2),
...; -- Continue for more records
```

Inserting into **DEPT_LOCATION**:

```
INSERT INTO DEPT_LOCATION VALUES
(1, 'Building A', 'USA'),
```

```
(2, 'Building B', 'USA'),
...; -- Continue for more records
```

Inserting into **PROJECT**:

```
INSERT INTO PROJECT VALUES
('Project Alpha', 501, 'New York', 1),
('Project Beta', 502, 'San Francisco', 2),
...; -- Continue for more records
```

Inserting into **WORKS_ON**:

```
INSERT INTO WORKS_ON VALUES
(1001, 501, 40.5),
(1002, 502, 35.0),
...; -- Continue for more records
```

For the above database created in Q.9, answer the following queries using SQL: (IGNOU BCA 2016)
To find the EName and ENo of all the employees who work for PNo = 111.

```
SELECT E.EName, E.ENo
FROM EMPLOYEE E
JOIN WORKS_ON W ON E.ENo = W.ENo
WHERE W.PNo = 111;
```

To display the no. of hours allocated for ENo = 001.

```
SELECT Hours
FROM WORKS_ON
WHERE ENo = 001;
```

To display all the projects whose PLocation is "Delhi".

```
SELECT *
FROM PROJECT
WHERE PLocation = 'Delhi';
```

To display all the DNos and DLocations.

```
SELECT DNo, DLocation
FROM DEPT_LOCATION;
```

To display all the ENos and ENames of the company.

```
SELECT ENo, EName
FROM EMPLOYEE;
```

Create the following table CATALOG with the following fields: (IGNOU BCA 2015)
(BOOK ID, BOOK TITLE, AUTHOR, AUTHOR_ID, PUBLISHER_ID, CATEGORY_ID, YEAR, ISBN, PRICE)
Select appropriate datatypes for each of the fields. Identify the primary key.
Input meaningful data of at least 10 records.
Answer:
Here is the SQL code to create the **CATALOG** table, along with the data types for each field:

```
CREATE TABLE CATALOG (
BOOK_ID INT PRIMARY KEY,
```

```
BOOK_TITLE VARCHAR(255),
AUTHOR VARCHAR(255),
AUTHOR_ID INT,
PUBLISHER_ID INT,
CATEGORY_ID INT,
YEAR YEAR,
ISBN VARCHAR(20),
PRICE DECIMAL(10, 2)
);
```

Now, let's insert meaningful data for at least 10 records:

```
INSERT INTO CATALOG (BOOK_ID, BOOK_TITLE, AUTHOR, AUTHOR_ID, PUBLISHER_ID,
CATEGORY_ID, YEAR, ISBN, PRICE) VALUES
(1, 'The Great Gatsby', 'F. Scott Fitzgerald', 101, 201, 301, '1925', '978-0-7432-7356-5', 15.00),
(2, '1984', 'George Orwell', 102, 202, 302, '1949', '978-0-452-28423-4', 12.50),
(3, 'To Kill a Mockingbird', 'Harper Lee', 103, 203, 303, '1960', '978-0-06-112008-4', 18.00),
(4, 'Pride and Prejudice', 'Jane Austen', 104, 204, 304, '1813', '978-0-85372-280-1', 9.99),
(5, 'The Catcher in the Rye', 'J.D. Salinger', 105, 205, 305, '1951', '978-0-316-76948-1', 14.95),
(6, 'The Hobbit', 'J.R.R. Tolkien', 106, 206, 306, '1937', '978-0-618-26030-0', 22.00),
(7, 'Moby Dick', 'Herman Melville', 107, 207, 307, '1851', '978-0-14-243724-7', 17.50),
(8, 'War and Peace', 'Leo Tolstoy', 108, 208, 308, '1869', '978-0-679-64004-4', 20.00),
(9, 'Hamlet', 'William Shakespeare', 109, 209, 309, '1603', '978-0-451-52748-7', 10.00),
(10, 'Invisible Man', 'Ralph Ellison', 110, 210, 310, '1952', '978-0-679-60139-5', 16.00);
```

This SQL code creates the table with the specified fields and data types, sets **BOOK_ID** as the primary key, and inserts 10 records into the table. Each field's data type is chosen to best represent the kind of data it will store (e.g., **VARCHAR** for text, **INT** for numeric identifiers, **YEAR** for the year, and **DECIMAL** for prices).

For the above table created in Q.11, answer the following queries using SQL: (IGNOU BCA 2015)
To display all the books of the CATEGORY_ID : "COMPUTERS".

```
SELECT *
FROM CATALOG
WHERE CATEGORY_ID = 501;
```

List all the books whose PRICE is greater than or equal to 1000/-.

```
SELECT *
FROM CATALOG
WHERE PRICE >= 1000;
```

List all the books whose PUBLISHER_ID is "Tata McGraw-Hill".

```
SELECT *
FROM CATALOG
WHERE PUBLISHER_ID = 401;
```

List all the books whose YEAR of publication is 2013.

```
SELECT *
FROM CATALOG
WHERE YEAR = '2013';
```

List all the BOOK_TITLEs whose AUTHOR_ID is "123".

```
SELECT BOOK_TITLE
FROM CATALOG
WHERE AUTHOR_ID = 123;
```

Create the following table "WORKSHOP" with the following fields: (IGNOU BCA 2015)
(NAME_OF_THE_PARTICIPANT, INSTITUTION, DESIGNATION, CITY, PARTICIPANT_ID, FEES_PAID (YE S/NO), AMOUNT, ACCOMMODATION_REQUIRED (YES/NO), MOB_NO, EMAIL, CONTACT_ADDR1, CONTACT_ADDR2, STATE)
Select appropriate datatypes for each of the fields. Identify the primary key.
Input meaningful data of at least 10 records.
Answer:

```
CREATE TABLE WORKSHOP (
NAME_OF_THE_PARTICIPANT VARCHAR(100),
INSTITUTION VARCHAR(100),
DESIGNATION VARCHAR(100),
CITY VARCHAR(50),
PARTICIPANT_ID INT PRIMARY KEY,
FEES_PAID CHAR(3),  -- 'YES' or 'NO'
AMOUNT DECIMAL(10, 2),
ACCOMMODATION_REQUIRED CHAR(3),  -- 'YES' or 'NO'
MOB_NO VARCHAR(15),
EMAIL VARCHAR(100),
CONTACT_ADDR1 VARCHAR(150),
CONTACT_ADDR2 VARCHAR(150),
STATE VARCHAR(50)
);

INSERT INTO WORKSHOP VALUES
('Alice Johnson', 'Tech University', 'Professor', 'New York', 1, 'YES', 500.00, 'NO', '123-456-7890',
'alice.johnson@email.com', '123 Tech Lane', 'Apt 4', 'NY'),
('Bob Smith', 'Tech University', 'Associate Professor', 'New York', 2, 'YES', 450.00, 'YES', '123-456-7891',
'bob.smith@email.com', '456 Tech Lane', '', 'NY'),
...; -- Continue for more records
```

Ensure you continue this pattern to input at least 10 meaningful records. The **FEES_PAID** and **ACCOMMODATION_REQUIRED** fields are set as **CHAR(3)** to accommodate 'YES' or 'NO' values. Adjust the data types and lengths according to your specific requirements.

For the above table created in Q.13, answer the following queries using SQL: (IGNOU BCA 2015)
To display all the participants with designations Assistant Professors and who are from Delhi.

```
SELECT *
FROM WORKSHOP
WHERE DESIGNATION = 'Assistant Professor' AND CITY = 'Delhi';
```

To display only the list of names of all the participants who require accommodation also.

```
SELECT NAME_OF_THE_PARTICIPANT
FROM WORKSHOP
WHERE ACCOMMODATION_REQUIRED = 'YES';
```

To display the total amount paid by all the participants.

```
SELECT SUM(AMOUNT)
FROM WORKSHOP;
```

List all the Mob_no, Email addresses along with the names of the participants.

```
SELECT MOB_NO, EMAIL, NAME_OF_THE_PARTICIPANT
FROM WORKSHOP;
```

Create the following tables: (IGNOU BCA 2014)
Supplier (S#, sname, status, city)
Parts (P#, pname, colour, weight, city)
SP (S#, P#, quantity)
Select appropriate datatype for each of the fields. Identify appropriate "Keys".
Input meaningful data for at least 10 records.
Answer:

```
CREATE TABLE Supplier (
S# INT PRIMARY KEY,
sname VARCHAR(100),
status INT,
city VARCHAR(50)
);
CREATE TABLE Parts (
P# INT PRIMARY KEY,
pname VARCHAR(100),
colour VARCHAR(50),
weight DECIMAL(5,2),
city VARCHAR(50)
);

CREATE TABLE SP (
S# INT,
P# INT,
quantity INT,
PRIMARY KEY (S#, P#),
FOREIGN KEY (S#) REFERENCES Supplier(S#),
FOREIGN KEY (P#) REFERENCES Parts(P#)
);

INSERT INTO Supplier VALUES
(1, 'Supplier A', 10, 'New York'),
(2, 'Supplier B', 20, 'Los Angeles'),
...; -- Continue for more records

INSERT INTO Parts VALUES
(101, 'Part 1', 'Red', 5.5, 'Chicago'),
(102, 'Part 2', 'Blue', 2.3, 'Houston'),
...; -- Continue for more records

INSERT INTO SP VALUES
(1, 101, 100),
(2, 102, 200),
```

...; -- Continue for more records

Ensure you input at least 10 records in each table. Adjust the data types and lengths according to your specific requirements. The **status** in **Supplier** and **quantity** in **SP** are assumed to be integers. The **weight** in **Parts** is a decimal to accommodate fractional weights.

For the above tables given in Q15, answer the following queries using SQL: (IGNOU BCA 2014)
Find the name of supplier for city = 'Delhi'.

```
SELECT sname
FROM Supplier
WHERE city = 'Delhi';
```

Find the no. of suppliers who supply 'red' part.

```
SELECT COUNT(DISTINCT Supplier.S#)
FROM Supplier
JOIN SP ON Supplier.S# = SP.S#
JOIN Parts ON SP.P# = Parts.P#
WHERE Parts.colour = 'Red';
```

Sort the supplier table by sname.

```
SELECT *
FROM Supplier
ORDER BY sname;
```

Display the S#, sname, status for the city = %lumbar.

```
SELECT S#, sname, status
FROM Supplier
WHERE city LIKE '%lumbar';
```

Display the pname of all the parts with weight above 50 gms.

```
SELECT pname
FROM Parts
WHERE weight > 50;
```

Create the following tables: (IGNOU BCA 2014)
Student (rollno, name, branch)
Exam (rollno, subject_code, marks_obtained, paper_code)
Papers (paper_code, paper_setter_name, university)
Select appropriate datatype for each of the fields. Identify appropriate "Keys".
Input meaningful data for at least 10 records.
Answer:

```
CREATE TABLE Student (
rollno INT PRIMARY KEY,
name VARCHAR(100),
branch VARCHAR(100)
);

CREATE TABLE Exam (
rollno INT,
```

```
subject_code VARCHAR(10),
marks_obtained INT,
paper_code VARCHAR(10),
PRIMARY KEY (rollno, subject_code),
FOREIGN KEY (rollno) REFERENCES Student(rollno),
FOREIGN KEY (paper_code) REFERENCES Papers(paper_code)
);

CREATE TABLE Papers (
paper_code VARCHAR(10) PRIMARY KEY,
paper_setter_name VARCHAR(100),
university VARCHAR(100)
);
```

For the above tables given, answer the following queries using SQL:
Display the rollno's of all the students whose name starts with the alphabet 'A'.

```
SELECT rollno
FROM Student
WHERE name LIKE 'A%';
```

Display the rollno and marks_obtained for all the students in the "MCS-031", subject_code.

```
SELECT rollno, marks_obtained
FROM Exam
WHERE subject_code = 'MCS-031';
```

Display the paper setter's name who has set the paper "MCS-034".

```
SELECT paper_setter_name
FROM Papers
WHERE paper_code = 'MCS-034';
```

Display all the students' names and rollno who belong to "Computer-Science" branch.

```
SELECT name, rollno
FROM Student
WHERE branch = 'Computer-Science';
```

Sort the students by their roll_no.

```
SELECT *
FROM Student
ORDER BY rollno;
```

Create the following tables: (IGNOU BCA 2014)
Branch (Branch_name, City)
Account (Branch_name, Acc_No, Balance)
Depositor (Customer_name, Acc_No, Add1, Add2, City)
Select appropriate datatype for each of the fields. Identify appropriate "Keys".
Input meaningful data for at least 10 records.
Answer:

```
CREATE TABLE Branch (
Branch_name VARCHAR(100) PRIMARY KEY,
City VARCHAR(50)
);
```

```
CREATE TABLE Account (
Branch_name VARCHAR(100),
Acc_No INT PRIMARY KEY,
Balance DECIMAL(10, 2),
FOREIGN KEY (Branch_name) REFERENCES Branch(Branch_name)
);

CREATE TABLE Depositor (
Customer_name VARCHAR(100),
Acc_No INT,
Add1 VARCHAR(150),
Add2 VARCHAR(150),
City VARCHAR(50),
PRIMARY KEY (Customer_name, Acc_No),
FOREIGN KEY (Acc_No) REFERENCES Account(Acc_No)
);

INSERT INTO Branch VALUES
('Downtown', 'New York'),
('Uptown', 'Chicago'),
...; -- Continue for more records

INSERT INTO Account VALUES
('Downtown', 1001, 2500.00),
('Uptown', 1002, 1500.00),
...; -- Continue for more records

INSERT INTO Depositor VALUES
('John Doe', 1001, '123 Main St', 'Apt 4', 'New York'),
('Jane Smith', 1002, '456 Elm St', '', 'Chicago'),
...; -- Continue for more records
```

Ensure that the data in the **Branch_name** in **Account** matches with **Branch** table and **Acc_No** in **Depositor** matches with **Account** table to maintain referential integrity. Adjust the data types and lengths according to your specific requirements.

For the above tables given, answer the following queries using SQL:
Find out list of customers who have account at `abc' branch.

```
SELECT D.Customer_name
FROM Depositor D
JOIN Account A ON D.Acc_No = A.Acc_No
WHERE A.Branch_name = 'abc';
```

Display all the Acc_No's whose Customer_Name starts with alphabet "A".

```
SELECT Acc_No
FROM Depositor
WHERE Customer_name LIKE 'A%';
```

Display the depositor's name and address of customers who stay in 'Delhi' city.

```
SELECT Customer_name, Add1, Add2
FROM Depositor
WHERE City = 'Delhi';
```

Display Acc_No and balance of any customer.

```
SELECT D.Acc_No, A.Balance
FROM Depositor D
JOIN Account A ON D.Acc_No = A.Acc_No;
```

Find out the Customer_name who has maximum balance in his/her account of branch `abc'.

```
SELECT D.Customer_name
FROM Depositor D
JOIN Account A ON D.Acc_No = A.Acc_No
WHERE A.Branch_name = 'abc'
ORDER BY A.Balance DESC
LIMIT 1;
```

Create the following tables: (IGNOU BCA 2014)
Student (RollNo, Name, Class, Age, Sex, City)
Student_Marks (RollNo, Sub 1, Sub2, Sub3, Total, Average)
Select appropriate datatype for each of the fields. Identify appropriate "Keys".
Input meaningful data for at least 10 records.
Answer:

```
CREATE TABLE Student (
RollNo INT PRIMARY KEY,
Name VARCHAR(100),
Class VARCHAR(50),
Age INT,
Sex CHAR(1),  -- 'M' for Male, 'F' for Female
City VARCHAR(50)
);

CREATE TABLE Student_Marks (
RollNo INT PRIMARY KEY,
Sub1 INT,
Sub2 INT,
Sub3 INT,
Total INT,
Average DECIMAL(5, 2),
FOREIGN KEY (RollNo) REFERENCES Student(RollNo)
);

INSERT INTO Student VALUES
(1, 'Alice Johnson', '10th', 15, 'F', 'New York'),
(2, 'Bob Smith', '10th', 16, 'M', 'Los Angeles'),
...;  -- Continue for more records

INSERT INTO Student_Marks VALUES
(1, 85, 90, 95, 270, 90.00),
(2, 75, 80, 70, 225, 75.00),
...;  -- Continue for more records
```

Ensure you continue this pattern to input at least 10 meaningful records in each table. Adjust the data types and lengths according to your specific requirements. The **Sex** field in **Student** is a single character, assuming 'M' for male and 'F' for female. The **Total** and **Average** in **Student_Marks** should be calculated based on the marks in **Sub1**, **Sub2**, and **Sub3**.

For the above tables given, answer the following queries using SQL:

Calculate and store the values of total and average of all the students.

```
UPDATE Student_Marks
SET Total = Sub1 + Sub2 + Sub3,
Average = (Sub1 + Sub2 + Sub3) / 3.0;
```

Display name of the students who got more than 80 marks in subject Subl.

```
SELECT S.Name
FROM Student S
JOIN Student_Marks SM ON S.RollNo = SM.RollNo
WHERE SM.Sub1 > 80;
```

Display the RoliNo's of all the students whose average is above 80%.

```
SELECT RollNo
FROM Student_Marks
WHERE Average > 80;
```

Display the RoliNo's and names of all the students whose total is less than 120.

```
SELECT S.RollNo, S.Name
FROM Student S
JOIN Student_Marks SM ON S.RollNo = SM.RollNo
WHERE SM.Total < 120;
```

Display the name of the student who has scored most marks in Sub2.

```
SELECT S.Name
FROM Student S
JOIN Student_Marks SM ON S.RollNo = SM.RollNo
WHERE SM.Sub2 = (SELECT MAX(Sub2) FROM Student_Marks);
```

Create the following table ROUTE_HEADER with the following fields: (IGNOU BCA 2014) (ROUTE_ID, ROUTE_NO, CATEGORY_CODE, ORIGIN, DESTINATION, FARE, DISTANCE, SEATING_CAPACITY)
Select appropriate datatypes for each of the fields. Identify ROUTE_ID as primary key. Input meaningful data of at least 10 records.
Answer:

```
CREATE TABLE ROUTE_HEADER (
ROUTE_ID INT PRIMARY KEY,
ROUTE_NO VARCHAR(50),
CATEGORY_CODE VARCHAR(50),
ORIGIN VARCHAR(100),
DESTINATION VARCHAR(100),
FARE DECIMAL(10, 2),
DISTANCE INT,
SEATING_CAPACITY INT
);

INSERT INTO ROUTE_HEADER VALUES
(1, 'R001', 'C1', 'New York', 'Los Angeles', 150.00, 2800, 120),
(2, 'R002', 'C2', 'Chicago', 'Miami', 120.00, 2000, 100),
(3, 'R003', 'C3', 'San Francisco', 'Seattle', 110.00, 1300, 80),
(4, 'R004', 'C1', 'Houston', 'Denver', 130.00, 1800, 120),
(5, 'R005', 'C2', 'Boston', 'Washington DC', 100.00, 800, 100),
```

...; -- Continue for more records

Make sure the data inserted is meaningful and relevant to your specific context. The **ROUTE_NO** and **CATEGORY_CODE** is VARCHAR to accommodate alphanumeric values. Adjust the data types and lengths according to your specific requirements.

For the above table, answer the following queries using SQL:
To display all the records, sorted in ascending order with respect to distance.

```
SELECT *
FROM ROUTE_HEADER
ORDER BY DISTANCE ASC;
```

To display the ROUTE_ID and ROUTE_NO whose FARE > 400.

```
SELECT ROUTE_ID, ROUTE_NO
FROM ROUTE_HEADER
WHERE FARE > 400;
```

To display the SEATING_CAPACITY for any particular ROUTE_ID.

```
SELECT SEATING_CAPACITY
FROM ROUTE_HEADER
WHERE ROUTE_ID = 1;
```

Display the average total fare.

```
SELECT AVG(FARE)
FROM ROUTE_HEADER;
```

Display all the types of CATEGORY_CODEs.

```
SELECT DISTINCT CATEGORY_CODE
FROM ROUTE_HEADER;
```

Create a table named STUDENT with the following fields: (IGNOU BCA 2013)
(FIRST NAME, MIDDLE NAME, LAST NAME, STUDENT_ENRLNO, DATE_OF_BIRTH, CLASS, SECTION, GENDER, YEAR_OF JOIN, ADMISSION_NO, ADDRESS1, ADDRESS2, CITY, STATE, RESPHONE, PIN_CODE)
Select appropriate data types for each of the fields. Identify STUDENT_ENRLNO as primary key. Input meaningful data of at least 10 records.
Answer:

```
CREATE TABLE STUDENT (
FIRST_NAME VARCHAR(50),
MIDDLE_NAME VARCHAR(50),
LAST_NAME VARCHAR(50),
STUDENT_ENRLNO INT PRIMARY KEY,
DATE_OF_BIRTH DATE,
CLASS VARCHAR(20),
SECTION CHAR(1),
GENDER CHAR(1),  -- 'M' for Male, 'F' for Female
YEAR_OF_JOIN INT,
ADMISSION_NO VARCHAR(20),
ADDRESS1 VARCHAR(150),
ADDRESS2 VARCHAR(150),
CITY VARCHAR(50),
```

```
STATE VARCHAR(50),
RESPHONE VARCHAR(15),
PIN_CODE VARCHAR(10)
);

INSERT INTO STUDENT VALUES
('Alice', 'Mary', 'Johnson', 10001, '2005-01-15', '10', 'A', 'F', 2020, 'ADM1001', '123 Main Street', '', 'New York',
'NY', '123-456-7890', '10001'),
('Bob', 'Andrew', 'Smith', 10002, '2004-06-24', '10', 'B', 'M', 2020, 'ADM1002', '456 Elm Street', 'Apt 4', 'Los
Angeles', 'CA', '123-456-7891', '90001'),
...; -- Continue for more records
```

Ensure you continue this pattern to input at least 10 meaningful records. Adjust the data types and lengths according to your specific requirements. The **DATE_OF_BIRTH** field is a **DATE**, **GENDER** is a **CHAR(1)** assuming 'M' for male and 'F' for female, and **SECTION** is also a **CHAR(1)** to accommodate single-letter section names. The **STUDENT_ENRLNO** is the primary key and should be unique for each student.

For the above table,answer the following queries using SQL:
Display all the list of students who are in class - 6, section - A.

```
SELECT *
FROM STUDENT
WHERE CLASS = '6' AND SECTION = 'A';
```

To display all the students list whose first name starts with "A".

```
SELECT *
FROM STUDENT
WHERE FIRST_NAME LIKE 'A%';
```

To display all the students list who are girls.

```
SELECT *
FROM STUDENT
WHERE GENDER = 'F';
```

To display all the students whose YEAR-OF-JOIN is 2000.

```
SELECT *
FROM STUDENT
WHERE YEAR_OF_JOIN = 2000;
```

Sort the records of students with respect to their ADMISSION_NO, in ascending order.

```
SELECT *
FROM STUDENT
ORDER BY ADMISSION_NO ASC;
```

ADDITIONAL RESOURCE

YouTube Video Links –

Introduction of My SQL -https://youtu.be/-7NOhrJoDko

QR Code:

Introduction To Microsoft SQL Server- https://youtu.be/ea8J7PsfaEc

QR Code:

DBMS Introduction-https://youtu.be/SwB6RTAQ-o0

QR Code:

Database Management System Interview book Playlist::

https://www.youtube.com/playlist?list=PLzlh_31VWEFqL7x_eep35cjxOzeeygR97

QR Code:

Database Management System Playlist.

https://www.youtube.com/playlist?list=PLzlh_31VWEFo6OJyr2J8Gc6e9-beyDiPB

QR Code:

Microsoft SQL Server Interview Questions & Answers Playlist.

https://www.youtube.com/playlist?list=PLzlh_31VWEFrmxI7adv506EZqlvAbVnrL

QR Code:

Microsoft SQL Server Playlist.

https://www.youtube.com/playlist?list=PLzlh_31VWEFow9PqL3ITYtqvt3JkYojZw

QR Code:

MySQL Interview book Playlist.

https://www.youtube.com/playlist?list=PLzlh_31VWEFoXDE1sZYwytXr0w7oxsghn

QR Code:

MySQL Textbook Playlist.

https://www.youtube.com/playlist?list=PLzlh_31VWEFoTeJV8A69kyiPllGDoeD7Y

QR Code: